IMAGES
of America

MOTOR CITY MAFIA
A CENTURY OF
ORGANIZED CRIME IN DETROIT

IMAGES
of America

MOTOR CITY MAFIA
A CENTURY OF
ORGANIZED CRIME IN DETROIT

Scott M. Burnstein

ARCADIA
PUBLISHING

Copyright © 2006 by Scott M. Burnstein
ISBN 978-0-7385-4084-9

Published by Arcadia Publishing
Charleston, South Carolina

Printed in the United States of America

Library of Congress Catalog Card Number: 2006924919

For all general information contact Arcadia Publishing at:
Telephone 843-853-2070
Fax 843-853-0044
E-mail sales@arcadiapublishing.com
For customer service and orders:
Toll-Free 1-888-313-2665

Visit us on the Internet at www.arcadiapublishing.com

CONTENTS

ACKNOWLEDGMENTS

I would like to dedicate this book to my grandmothers, Arlene and Lillian, and my grandfather, Sam. Special thanks to Mom, Dad, Grandpa Don (G-Money), Paul R. Kavieff, Mike Carone, Oscar Westerfield, Bill Randall, Bob Barenie, Joe Finnigan, Dave Parker, Adam Rafalski, Ty Spector (Jiggy), Mr. Green, Anna Wilson and Arcadia, Mary Wallace, Tom Featherstone and Wayne State, Ned Timmons, Richard Zuckerman, Norm Sinclair, Ian, Amy, Erin, David F., Sue, Neil Welch, Bobby B., Kathy, Jeremy, Jamie, Jake, Rachel, Tracey, Geri, David G., Stephanie, Sara, Morgan, Mac, Jeremy H., Eric, Judd, Rob, Andrew, Mikey, Rich, Eddie, John Binder, Ernie Righetti, Eric R., Byron, Laurie Evans, Nancy Webster, the Miller family, the Porter family, the Frank family, the Roeper family, the Glazek family, S. Owley, Jason, Dan, George Anastasia, the Butterscotch, the IU Nation, and the Detroit FBI office.

FOREWORD

Long before the 20th century and the advent of modern organized crime, Detroit had the reputation of being a rowdy river town. Under French, British, and, finally, American rule, smuggling, gambling, brothels, and other forms of vice flourished, and with the birth of the automobile industry the city of Detroit grew rapidly. From a population of several hundred thousand in the early 1900s, the city grew to be the fourth-largest metropolitan area in the country by 1927, with a population of almost two million people.

The great era of immigration, from 1880 to 1920, brought many thousands of eastern and southern Europeans to America looking for the opportunity to have a better life. The burgeoning Detroit automobile industry attracted many of these new Americans to Detroit to seek work in the booming automobile plants. Along with these newly arrived immigrants came many professional criminals. Some of these men had extensive criminal records in their country of origin. Unlike their hardworking and honest brethren, they came to America to prey on their fellow countrymen.

In Detroit, as in other cities, the first indication of this foreign criminal element came in the form of black hand gangs. The black hand extortion racket was a method employed by any criminal opportunist to squeeze money out of honest, hardworking people. Associated mostly with the southern Italian and Sicilian immigrant communities, so-called Black Handers sent intimidating letters to successful fellow countrymen, often imprinted with a black hand or dagger dripping blood. The letter threatened the victim or a family member with death if a tribute was not paid. In these immigrant communities, Black Handers were often considered to be members of the Sicilian Mafia or Neapolitan Camorra, two old-country criminal organizations that had been transplanted to America. To make the situation even more confusing, Mafia and Camorra gangs often used black hand extortion methods.

By the early 20th century, Detroit had its own Mafia gangs. First the Adamo and Gianolla brothers fought for control of the Italian lottery and extortion rackets in Detroit. During that struggle, the Gianolla brothers ambushed and killed the Adamo brothers and quickly rose to prominence. By the second decade of the 20th century, a faction of the Gianolla Mob had broken from the gang, led by a former Gianolla gunman named "John" Vitale. For a period of almost three years, a Mafia war raged between the Gianolla and Vitale Mobs on Detroit's lower east side. More than 100 men were killed in this gang war, which ended with the murder of John Vitale. Both Gianolla brothers were also killed in the strife. As a result, a former Gianolla gunman and diplomat, Salvatore Catalanotte, respected by both sides, rose to power. As a result, for a period of almost 10 years there was relative peace among the Mafia factions in Detroit.

During the second decade of the 20th century, a juvenile street gang was formed in the same lower east side Detroit neighborhood in which the Gianolla/Vitale gang war was raging. These predominantly Jewish hoodlums would later form the core group of the Detroit Purple Gang. The Purples would become one of the most infamous Prohibition-era organized crime groups.

With statewide Prohibition coming to Michigan in 1918 and national Prohibition in 1920, the Purple Gang was catapulted into power in the Detroit underworld. The Purples first built their ferocity as notorious hijackers of liquor shipments. The Cleaners and Dyers War, Milaflores Massacre, and Collingwood Massacre would mark the meteoric beginning, middle, and end of the Purple Gang's reign of terror. From 1927 to 1932, the Purple Gang ruled the Detroit underworld through fear and official protection. Led by the four Bernstein brothers, Abe, Joe, Ray, and Isadore, they controlled the local wire service that provided horse racing information to more than 700 handbooks that flourished in Detroit. The Purples also controlled illegal gambling, drugs, bootlegging, and prostitution. Any underworld operator doing business in Detroit during that time either kicked back money to the Purples or ceased to operate. Some 500 unsolved Prohibition-era murders have been attributed to the gang.

During this same period, the remnants of the old Gianolla and Vitale gangs formed an outfit known as the River Gang. This group was controlled by Joe Moceri, the Licavoli brothers, and other notorious Mafia gangsters. The River Gang ran a large-scale taxi service running liquor and beer into Michigan from Ontario, Canada. Operating north and south of Detroit during Prohibition, they controlled most of the illegal booze entering southeast Michigan from Canada. Large-scale smugglers on the United States side would contract with the River Gang to bring Canadian liquor and beer into Michigan. By the early 1920s, most of the large-scale liquor smuggling on the Detroit River was controlled by the River Gang. This outfit represented the true birth of the Detroit Mafia family.

By the early 1930s, the Purple Gang had begun to self-destruct, and the various Mafia factions in Detroit were once again at war with each other. Between 1930 and 1931, the Crosstown Mob Wars raged between the so-called East Side and West Side mobs, actually factions of the Detroit Mafia. The war began with the death of Salvatore Catalanotte in 1930. At the end of 1931, the modern Detroit Mafia family was born, led by Angelo Meli, Joseph Zerilli, William "Black Bill" Tocco, John Priziola, and Pete Licavoli. These men were all senior gunmen who got their start in the Gianolla/Vitale war and the River Gang. By 1935, the Detroit Mafia family controlled illegal gambling, drugs, loan sharking, prostitution, and the other profitable rackets once controlled by the Purple Gang.

There was very little ethnic rivalry in the Detroit underworld. There were no gang wars between the Purples and the Detroit Mafia. The Italian Mob just stepped into the void left by the implosion and self-destruction of the Purple Gang by 1935. The Purple Gang and the local Italian Mob were always on amiable terms. This was true for all but a few Purple Gang outlaws and freelancers like Harry Millman and his crew, who shook down Mafia-controlled handbooks and brothels. Millman paid for these infractions with his life when he was shot to death in a sensational murder in a Detroit restaurant in 1937.

Throughout the 1940s and 1950s, the Detroit Mafia consolidated its power in both Detroit and in Windsor, Ontario. With the millions made during Prohibition and from other lucrative rackets, they bought into legitimate businesses such as laundries, sanitation companies, restaurants, and construction. By the 1970s, the Detroit Mobs' major moneymaking operations were from horse race betting and illegal sports betting. They took in millions a year from the Detroit Mob–controlled Aladdin Casino in Las Vegas. Illegal money was often laundered through legitimate businesses. The Detroit Mafia remained relatively unscathed, due in part to its relatively low profile in the last decades of the 20th century. In 1996, federal Racketeer Influenced and Corrupt Organizations (RICO) indictments began to bring down the leadership of the Detroit Mob. By the late 1990s, Mafia turncoats in the Detroit family were beginning to erode the power of the Detroit Mafia.

In *Motor City Mafia: A Century of Organized Crime in Detroit*, crime historian Scott M. Burnstein, through photographic images, mug shots, surveillance, and crime scene photographs, introduces the reader to some of the most violent men in the history of U.S. organized crime.

This is a necessary book for any serious crime historian or reader who is interested in the dark side of Detroit history. It is the first book to photographically explore the history of the Detroit underworld.

Paul R. Kavieff
Royal Oak, Michigan
May 16, 2006

One

THE BEGINNING

At the beginning of the 20th century, America was changing—in culture, in industry, and, most of all, in size. Hoards of immigrants hailing from across the vast continent of Europe filled the streets of metropolitan cities and quickly made their presence felt in their new communities. The city of Detroit was one of the best examples of this phenomenon. By the end of the new century's first decade, Detroit was a melting pot of ethnicity and foreign culture, spawning several neighborhoods specific to Italian, Jewish, Polish, and Irish decent. With these new communities came old world–style traditions, brought by the influx of Europeans with them to their new country. These traditions ranged from the benign to the tremendously lethal, the most dangerous of which was the underground criminal society, known by many as "the Camorra" or "the Black Hand." Just like the many people from Italy and its tiny neighbor Sicily, who arrived in America, so did their tradition of a secret society of criminals, whose power equaled and in some cases even exceeded that of the elected government and would in later years become known as "the Mafia."

The first incarnation of this eerily mysterious fraternity in the city of Detroit, the forefather to what is today modern organized crime, was the Adamo Gang, which sprang up in 1905 and was lead by Tony and Vito Adamo. By 1910, all of the area's liquor distribution, gambling, loan sharking, prostitution, and extortion rings were under their control. In 1913, the Adamo Gang went to war with the Gianolla Gang, a faction of street toughs led by the Gianolla brothers. The Adamos were killed by Gianolla gunmen as the pair walked together on a city street corner, paving the way for the Gianolla's to assume control of the local underworld for themselves. In 1919, after six years of power, the Gianolla brothers were unseated by a former ally named John Vitale, who turned against his bosses and had them murdered. Vitale's rule was short-lived and he was killed by Gianolla loyalists within a year after taking power. With the onset of Prohibition, former Gianolla lieutenant Salvatore "Singing Sam" Catalanotte was elected gangland overlord of Detroit and maintained final authority over all activities regarding the city's newest criminal regimes, the Purple Gang, the River Gang, the East Side Gang, and the West Side Gang.

This is a Detroit Police Department (DPD) mug shot of early-20th-century Mob boss Sam Gianolla, who alongside his brother Tony wrestled control of the local underworld from previous city crime lords the Adamo Gang in 1913 and ruled the Motor City streets unchallenged for the next six years. Gianolla was gunned down and killed in October 1919 on the corner of Russell Street and Monroe Avenue by hit men sent by rival gang leader Giovanni "John" Vitale. (Walter Reuther Library—Wayne State University.)

This is a DPD mug shot of John Gianolla, first cousin to former city overlords the Gianolla brothers, who along with his brother Vito founded the notorious Green Ones Gang in St. Louis before coming to the Motor City in 1927 and going to work for the local Italian crime syndicate. (Walter Reuther Library—Wayne State University.)

DPD sergeant Emmanuel Rogers is pictured in this photograph taken in the early part of the 20th century. In 1917, Rogers, who was a leading member of the department's special squad in charge of taking down the city's street gangs, was murdered on the orders of the Gianolla brothers. (Paul R. Kavieff collection.)

This mug shot is of James (Jim) Vitale, younger brother of early-20th-century crime lord John Vitale, who along with his powerful older sibling played a major role in the city's first two gang wars. When John was killed by members of his own gang in the fall of 1920, Jim continued on in the local underworld as an enforcer under Prohibition-era Mob leader Salvatore "Singing Sam" Catalanotte. (Walter Reuther Library—Wayne State University.)

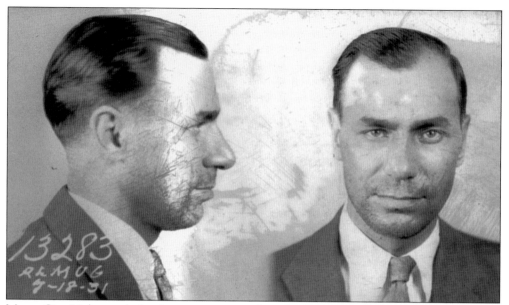

Motor City Mob muscle Joe Locano is pictured in this DPD mug shot taken after an arrest in 1931. Locano, alongside underworld battery mate Joe Amico, was tried and acquitted for the gangland assassination of Gaspare "the Peacemaker" Milazzo and Sam "Sasha" Parina as the pair waited at the Vernor Highway Fish Market for what they thought was to be a peace conference between themselves and rival gang leader Chester "Big Chet" La Mare. (Walter Reuther Library—Wayne State University.)

Detroit Mob hit man Joe Amico is shown in 1930 while in court on trial for the infamous "Vernor Highway Fish Market Murders," a gruesome double-homicide orchestrated by city crime boss Big Chet La Mare. Soon thereafter, Amico turned trader and aided rival gang powers in carrying out the murder of La Mare. A victim of a Mob-related death himself, Amico disappeared in 1937, killed by the area crime syndicate over a monetary dispute. (Walter Reuther Library—Wayne State University.)

Hamtramck-area Mob kingpin Big Chet La
Mare, alongside his wife, is seen in a family
photograph from the late 1920s. La Mare, who
was the leader of the city's infamous West Side
Gang, became Detroit's number one crime
boss in 1930 when he orchestrated the Vernor
Highway Fish Market Murders. However, Big
Chet's rule over the Motor City was short-lived,
and he was murdered by his own men in
January 1931. (Walter Reuther Library—Wayne
State University.)

Slain Detroit radio broadcaster Gerald Buckley is shown in a picture taken in the years before
his death at the hands of the Motor City underworld. Buckley was killed on July 23, 1930, while
sitting in the lobby of the La Salle Hotel following one of his many on-air rants against the local
crime syndicate. Upset with his attention-grabbing antics, the area Italian Mob ordered him to
be killed. (Walter Reuther Library—Wayne State University.)

This late-Prohibition-era lineup photograph is of members of both the Purple Gang, the city's premiere Jewish bootlegging cartel, and the River Gang, the area's top Italian booze-smuggling crew. Also pictured, intermingled among the notorious dual vice-factions, are several members of the local Polish crime syndicate. Pay special attention to: Joseph "Joe Scarface" Bommarito (No. 1), the River Gang's primary enforcer; Eddie Fletcher (No. 13) and Abe Axler (No. 16), who were two of the Purple Gang's best assassins, and who would both be murdered by their counterparts in the Jewish Mob; James "Blackie" Licavoli (No. 11), River Gang member and future Mafia boss in Cleveland; James Moceri (No. 12), Licavoli's first cousin and fellow River Ganger; and Chester Tutha (No. 9), one of Detroit's biggest independent crime lords of the time period, leading Hamtramck's Lizard Gang. (Walter Reuther Library—Wayne State University.)

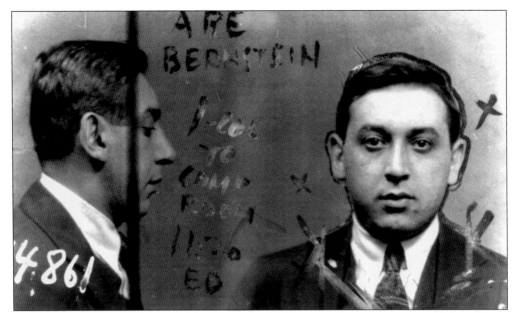

Purple Gang boss Abe Bernstein is pictured in a DPD mug shot from the early 1920s. Bernstein, along with his three brothers, built their Detroit-area Jewish crime syndicate into one of the most powerful, respected, and feared vice gangs in the annals of American history. Despite ruling less than a decade, the gang's legacy is long-standing as an iconic symbol of the local underworld. (Paul R. Kavieff collection.)

This early mug shot is of Detroit gang leader and future Motor City godfather Joseph "Joe Uno" Zerilli. Through the years, Zerilli would build a reputation second to none in the nation's underworld. During Prohibition he was a top member of the infamous East Side Gang. (Paul R. Kavieff collection.)

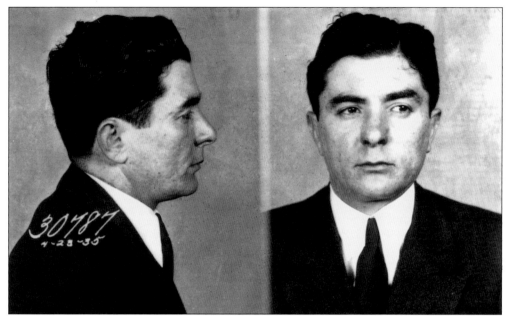

River Gang boss and future Detroit Mob chieftain Peter Licavoli is shown in a DPD mug shot taken in the mid-1930s. After Prohibition ended, Licavoli, originally from St. Louis and whose two brother-in-laws Joe Scarface Bommarito and Frank Cammerata were fellow gangland figures, was named a captain by Mafia boss Bill Tocco. (Paul R. Kavieff collection.)

Motor City Mob lieutenant Joe Scarface Bommarito is pictured sitting in court during his trial for the Gerald Buckley murder in the fall of 1930. A top member of the River Gang, Bommarito and his two codefendants were acquitted of all charges, and he went on to become a powerful Mafia captain in the newly formed Detroit crime family. Bommarito died of natural causes in 1965. (Walter Reuther—Wayne State University.)

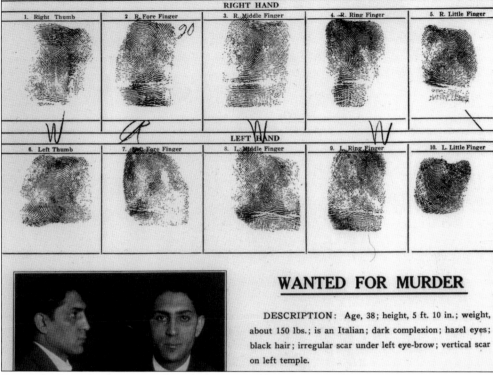

WANTED FOR MURDER

DESCRIPTION: Age, 38; height, 5 ft. 10 in.; weight, about 150 lbs.; is an Italian; dark complexion; hazel eyes; black hair; irregular scar under left eye-brow; vertical scar on left temple.

East Side Gang leader Leonardo "Black Leo" Cellura is pictured alongside his fingerprints in a 1930s DPD wanted poster that was displayed across the city in an attempt to apprehend the well-known fugitive. After nearly a decade on the run from the law, Cellura, who was wanted for murder and who, along with William "Black Bill" Tocco and Joseph "Joe Uno" Zerilli, founded and ran the highly feared East Side Gang, was caught and jailed and eventually died of natural causes in 1972 after his release. (Paul R. Kavieff collection.)

Detroit Mafia figure Joseph "Long Joe" Bommarito (second from left) is pictured alongside his first cousin Joe Scarface Bommarito (third from left) and Purple Gang associates David Feldman (next to Joe Scarface) and Dominic Licavoli (far right) in a DPD line-up photograph from the 1930s. Millman was notorious Purple enforcer Harry Millman's younger brother, while Long Joe would go on to become a powerful street lieutenant in the Motor City crime family and Feldman would become a highly-valued crime family associate. Also pictured in the photograph are local underworld figures Frank Cammerata and James Licavoli. (Paul R. Kavieff collection.)

17

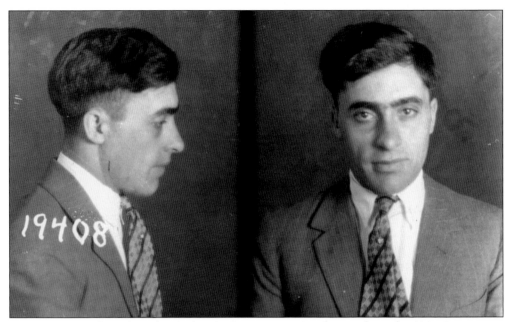

This police mug shot of Frank "Frankie C" Cammerata was taken in the early 1930s. Cammerata was a key member in the River Gang and one of the local underworld's most dreaded gunmen of the early century. Deported in 1937, Cammerata snuck back into the country in the 1940s, serving as the Detroit Mafia's representative in Toledo and Youngstown before dying of natural causes in 1965. (Paul R. Kavieff collection.)

Joseph "Joe Misery" Moceri, a coleader of the River Gang, is pictured leaving a court appearance in the late 1920s. After Prohibition, Moceri became a vital cog in the hierarchy of the city's Mafia crime family before succumbing to a violent death in August 1968, when he was killed by masked assailants in a robbery of a warehouse he owned in west Detroit. (Walter Reuther Library—Wayne State University.)

Joe Moceri (second from left), alongside several members of the River Gang, is pictured in this DPD lineup photograph from the late 1920s. Pay special attention to Calogero "Leo Lips" Moceri (third from left), Joe's younger brother, who would go on to become the underboss of the Cleveland Mafia in the 1970s and whose violent murder in 1976 would set off a bloody Mob war in Ohio that lasted close to two years. (Paul R. Kavieff collection.)

Former River Gang lieutenant and Detroit Mafia captain Joseph "Joe the Bum" Massei is pictured in a DPD mug shot from the early-Prohibition era. Getting his start under city crime lords the Gianolla brothers and then working as a trusted aid to Pete Licavoli, Massei was eventually appointed the syndicate's boss in charge of overseeing the family's interests in Florida. Massei died in 1972. (Paul R. Kavieff collection.)

This Prohibition-era photograph is of bootlegging activities taking place on the shores of the Detroit River, taken by the DPD and used as a diagram to demonstrate how alcoholic contraband was smuggled up the body of water from Canada on to U.S. territory and into a series of local underground speakeasies and Mob-run booze joints for illegal consumption. (Walter Reuther Library—Wayne State University.)

Stranded booze runners are on Lake St. Clair in the frigid winter of 1929. During Prohibition, the area's bootlegging gangs would transport large truckloads of black-market alcohol from Canada to the United States across the frozen lake water in the winter. Sometimes, as shown here, the weight of the delivery truck would break through the ice, leaving the smugglers and their shipments stuck in the lake. (Walter Reuther Library—Wayne State University.)

East Side Gang leaders and future Motor City Mob dons Joseph "Joe Uno" Zerilli (second from right) and William "Black Bill" Tocco (second from left) stand with detective William Delisle and prosecutor Frank Schemanski while being arraigned in the early 1930s. Zerilli and Tocco were brother-in-laws and best friends, aiding and counseling each other through their storied careers in the Detroit underworld. (Walter Reuther Library—Wayne State University.)

River Gang member and future local Mob lieutenant Thomas "Yonnie" Licavoli (left), younger brother of bootlegging czar Pete Licavoli, is pictured leaving court with his attorney. After Prohibition, Yonnie and his brother-in-law Frank Cammerata were dispensed by the Motor City Mafia to Toledo in order to look after the syndicate's interests in Ohio. Soon thereafter, Yonnie was imprisoned on murder charges. (Paul R. Kavieff collection.)

Located in the basement of this laundry on 10 Mile and Dequindre Roads on the city's east side was one of Detroit's numerous speakeasies, referred to locally as "blind pigs," these after-hours locales were top-secret underground booze joints run by the area crime syndicate offering spirits and good times to a thirsty public during the 1920s and early 1930s. (Walter Reuther Library—Wayne State University.)

Here is a look inside one of the city's most popular blind pig, located at the corner of Randolph and Columbia, during a busy night in the late 1920s. This particular establishment, owned and operated by the Purple Gang, was one of the most popular of the era. (Walter Reuther Library—Wayne State University.)

Two

THE PURPLE GANG

In the storied gangland history of the United States, the Purple Gang and its reign over the vast Detroit underworld landscape during the latter-part of the Prohibition era was an anomaly of epic-proportions—the heights they reached as a minority crime syndicate were never again equaled in the 75-plus years since the Purples controlled the Motor City's rackets. This small slice of local history, which lasted less than a decade and took place more than three quarters of a century previous, was a phenomenon so groundbreaking and sociologically influential that to this day the Purples stand as one of the most iconic figures in the annals of American crime. Taking their leadership from the four Bernstein brothers, the highly feared contingent of Jewish wiseguys ruled the city's streets with an iron fist from roughly 1925 through 1933, with authorities attributing to them over 500 area gangland slayings.

Forging a lucrative working relationships with the local Italian Mob syndicate and numerous other powerful vice gangs operating within the Midwest, the Purples controlled a large percentage of all the illegal alcohol flowing in and out of Detroit during Prohibition, as well as most of area's wire-service, prostitution, gambling, extortion, and narcotic rackets. Getting their moniker and namesake from a drugstore attendant the group of young Jewish criminals used to steal from, when she called them purple to a local newspaper reporter—at that time meaning off-white or tainted—the gang made national headlines when they helped Chicago gangster Al "Scarface" Capone orchestrate the infamous St. Valentine's Day Massacre in the Windy City. Following suit, they themselves pulled of the highly-polific Collingwood Manor Apartment Massacre in Detroit. At the end of Prohibition and following the convictions of three primary lieutenants in the gang as a result of the Collingwood trial, the Purples quietly and unceremoniously disbanded, with most of its members retiring from their lives in the underworld and going legitimate.

Abe Bernstein, Jewish Mob czar and founder of the infamous Purple Gang, is pictured alongside his attorney in the 1940s, during a local grand jury proceeding. After Prohibition ended, Bernstein got out of the rackets but maintained a steady allegiance to his various underworld associates until his death in the late 1960s. (Paul R. Kavieff collection.)

Purple Gang leader Joe Bernstein, younger brother of Abe, claimed his fortune came from running a tiny barbershop on the city's east side. A renowned dresser and ladies man, Joe was Abe's top emissary, eventually retiring from his life in crime and moving to California. (Paul R. Kavieff collection.)

Purple Gang leader Ray Bernstein, another younger brother of syndicate boss Abe, acted as the crime conglomerate's chief enforcer, making certain nobody dared muscle in on the Purple's rackets. Jailed for his participation in the highly publicized Collingwood Apartment Massacre, Ray spent almost 30 years in state prison, dying shortly after his release in the 1960s. (Paul R. Kavieff collection.)

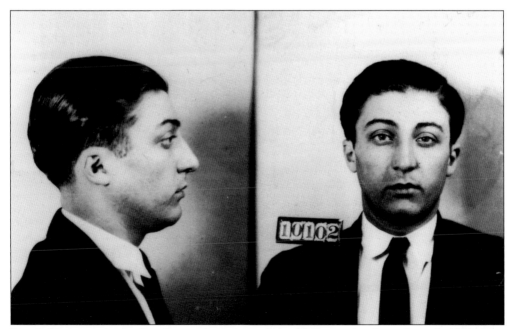

Purple Gang member Isadore Bernstein is pictured in a DPD mug shot from the early 1930s. The youngest of Abe's brothers, "Izzy", as his friends called him, was the least criminally talented of the infamous Bernsteins and following Prohibition retired to California with his brother Joe. (Paul R. Kavieff collection.)

This press photograph is of a late-1920s Detroit police raid on a local underground brewery on the city's east side. The dumping of the confiscated alcohol out the window onto the street, pictured in the image, was a common technique employed by the authorities in combating the many black-market distilleries and brewing factories that sprang up in record numbers throughout Prohibition. (Walter Reuther Library—Wayne State University.)

Purple Gang associate Samuel "Uncle Sam" Garfield is pictured in a press photograph from the 1950s. A close friend of the Bernstein brothers, Garfield acted as the conduit between the Purples and the East Coast underworld, specifically Meyer Lansky. Following the Jewish crime gang's disbandment, Garfield, who co-owned a lucrative oil company with Joe Bernstein, continued in the same capacity working for Detroit's Italian Mafia. (Paul R. Kavieff collection.)

Detroit's legendary Book Cadillac Hotel is shown as it looked in the late 1920s, when it acted as the headquarters of the notorious Purple Gang and its leaders, the highly feared Bernstein brothers. Holding court in the bar or coffee shop, Jewish Mob boss and Purple chief Abe Bernstein was a fixture at the popular hotel, maintaining a residence on the top floor until his death there in 1968. (Walter Reuther Library—Wayne State University.)

Purple gangsters Izzy Bernsetin (center, table) and Ray Bernsetin (right, corner of table) are shown while in court during their February 1930 trial on concealed weapons charges. In a widely covered trial by the local press, the notorious duo of brothers were acquitted of all charges and set free from state custody. (Walter Reuther Library—Wayne State University.)

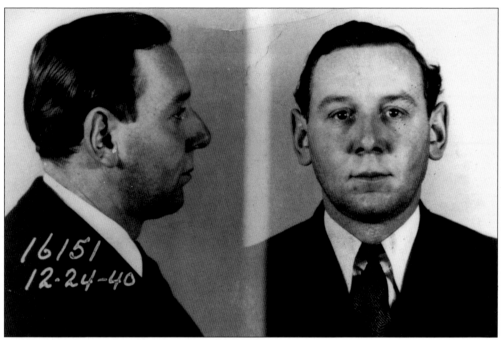

Purple Gang lieutenant Harry "H. F." Fleisher, one of the three notorious Fleisher brothers, is pictured in a police mug shot from 1940. Fleisher was best friends with Joe and Ray Bernstein, having known each other since they were small children. (Paul R. Kavieff collection.)

Infamous Purple Gang duo Sam "Sammy Purple" Cohen and Sam "Sammy K" Kert are pictured in a DPD mug shot, following an arrest in the early 1930s. Known on the streets as "the Two Sammies," Cohen and Kert forged a successful underworld business partnership while owning and operating a large portion of the gang's after-hours drinking establishments. (Walter Reuther Library—Wayne State University.)

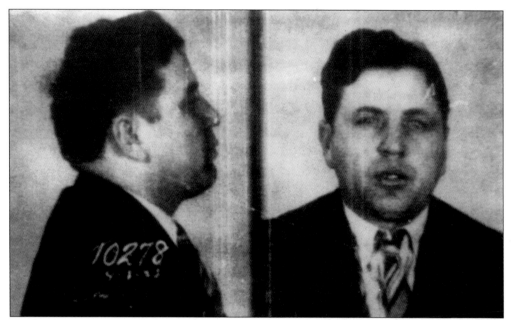

Oakland Sugar House Gang boss Henry Shorr is pictured in a DPD mug shot from the 1920s. The largest producer of sugar corn syrup—the primary ingredient in black-market booze—in the state, Shorr and his partner, Charles Leiter, mentored the Bernsteins as they got their start in the local underworld. Short had a falling-out with his proteges and was killed in December 1934 by Purple assassins. (Paul R. Kavieff collection.)

Much-feared Purple Gang enforcer Harry Millman is pictured in a DPD mug shot from the early 1930s. A member of what was dubbed "the Junior Purples," a rising young faction of Jewish wiseguys that came up on the Detroit streets and were schooled on the ways of the underworld by the Bernsteins, Millman went on to become the gang's top strong-arm. (Burton Historical Collection—Detroit Public Library.)

A reputed St. Valentine's Day Massacre gunman and Purple Gang associate, Fred "the Killer" Burke is shown in a mug shot from the late 1920s. A former member of the Egan's Rats Gang, a top St. Louis crime syndicate, Burke was reportedly dispatched, along with several others, by Purple boss Abe Bernstein to Chicago in the winter of 1929 to aid Windy City gang leader Al "Scarface" Capone in winning a local street war, which culminated in the nationally infamous St. Valentines Day Massacre on February 14, 1929. (Paul R. Kavieff collection.)

This photograph is of the Collingwood Manor apartment complex on Collingwood Avenue in East Detroit as it looked at the time of the Collingwood Massacre in September 1931. A boardinghouse for area residents and out-of-state travelers alike, the Collingwood was used by the Purple Gang as the site of the city's most infamous mass murder ever. (Walter Reuther Library—Wayne State University.)

This crime scene photograph is of Collingwood Massacre victim Isadore "Izzy the Rat" Sutker, pictured lying dead on the floor of apartment 211. One of the members of an offspring faction of the Purple Gang, who called themselves the Little Jewish Navy, Sutker and his associates tried in vain to take a piece of the area liquor rackets for themselves, before being killed on the orders of Abe Bernstein. (Walter Reuther Library—Wayne State University.)

This crime scene photograph is of Collingwood Massacre victims Joseph "Nigger Joe" Leibowitz (with feet showing) and Hymie Paul (body against wall), pictured lying dead shortly after being killed by Purple assassins Harry Keywell and Irving Milberg. Summoned to the Collingwood by Ray Bernstein for a meeting, the trio of subversives was gunned down as Bernstein waited in a getaway car outside. (Walter Reuther Library—Wayne State University.)

This crime scene photograph shows all three Collingwood Massacre victims sprawled out, face down on the floor of apartment 211. Notice Sutker (left) was killed while trying to climb underneath the bed, as Paul (foreground) and Leibowitz (background) were killed while making a run for the door. The only survivor of the brazen attack was Purple associate Sol Levine, who went onto testify against the three assailants in court. (Walter Reuther Library—Wayne State University.)

Shown is a press photograph of Purple Gang members and homicide suspects Ray Bernstein (center), Harry Keywell (right of Bernstein), and Irving Milberg (left of Bernstein) as they are being arraigned for the Collingwood murders. Tried and found guilty, the three Purple hit men were sentenced to lengthy state prison terms, effectively ending each of their careers in the local underworld. (Walter Reuther Library—Wayne State University.)

Three

THE COMBINATION

After 10 years of stability at the top of the city's criminal food chain, in January 1930, longtime Detroit Mob chieftain Sam Catalanotte died, and soon thereafter, various area gangland factions, each eager to fill the vacuum of power left by Catalanotte's passing, began a violent struggle for underworld supremacy. The East Side Gang, led by William "Black Bill" Tocco, Joseph "Joe Uno" Zerilli, and Angelo Meli and the West Side Gang, led by Chester "Big Chet" La Mare, squared off throughout the early part of 1930, setting the local streets ablaze with war for the first time in a decade. Soon New York crime lord Salvatore "Little Caesar" Maranzano stepped in and dispatched associate Gaspare "the Peacemaker" Milazzo to the Motor City to mediate the dispute and arrange a truce. On May 31, 1930, Milazzo and Sam "Sasha" Parina, an East Side Gang soldier, were ambushed by rival gunmen and killed at the Vernor Highway Fish Market, a popular area restaurant and meeting place, as they waited for the West Siders to arrive for an alleged peace conference, placing Big Chet La Mare alone atop the Detroit underworld.

Less than a year later, in February 1931, La Mare was killed by his own men in a murder plot devised by his East Side rivals, paving the way for the formation of the city's modern-day Mafia crime family. The conclusion of a large-scale East Coast Mob war, where several aging Sicilian dons were violently overthrown by a faction of young mafioso led by Charles "Lucky" Lucciano, brought immediate change to the U.S. underworld. At a gangland summit held in Chicago in the summer of 1931, Lucciano installed a brand-new nationwide criminal hierarchy known as La Cosa Nostra ("this thing of ours"), and the stage was set for a new beginning. The Motor City fell in-line behind Luccian and immediately consolidated all of its individual street gangs into one supreme crime syndicate, referred to locally as "the Combination" or "the Partnership," and elected Bill Tocco its first boss. In turn, Tocco then selected his brother-in-law and best friend Joe Zerilli as his underboss, or second in command, and Angelo Meli as his consiglieri, the crime family's official counselor or third in charge.

Motor City Mob don William "Black Bill" Tocco (left) and his attorney are shown following a court proceeding in the early 1930s. Tocco, who was a leader of the infamous East Side Gang, was selected to head the area's first incarnation of what is today the contemporary Detroit Mafia. (Walter Reuther Library—Wayne State University.)

Legendary Motor City godfather Joseph "Joe Uno" Zerilli is pictured in a photograph from 1931. Taking the reins of the city's crime family when Bill Tocco was jailed in 1936 for tax evasion, Zerilli held the position for over 40 years. Known on the streets as "Joe Peppino" or "the Old Man," Zerilli owned several legitimate businesses, including the Detroit Baking Company and Hazel Park Racetrack, and became an underworld superpower, serving on the Mafia's national commission. (Walter Reuther Library—Wayne State University.)

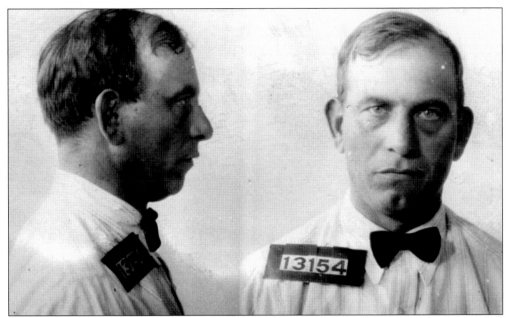

Joe Tocco, older brother of Detroit Mob boss Bill Tocco, is seen in a mug shot taken in the early 1930s. Before joining forces with his brother, Joe headed his own smaller bootlegging cartel out of the city's downriver area. However, the brothers soon merged interests, with Joe assuming a top position in his brother's administration until his death in 1938, when he was shot on the porch of his girlfriend's house. (Walter Reuther Library—Wayne State University.)

Sam Zerilli, younger brother of city crime lord Joe Zerilli, is shown in a DPD mug shot taken in the early 1930s. Sam served as a top lieutenant in his brother's administration and married off his daughter to fellow crime family member Peter "Bozzi" Vitale. (Walter Reuther Library—Wayne State University.)

Joe Zerilli and Bill Tocco are shown in a photograph taken at the DPD in the early 1930s. Tocco and Zerilli ruled the city's underworld side by side for a large portion of the century drawing acclaimed administration from their gangland colleagues across the nation. Notice the DPD's misspelling of the future godfather's last name. (Paul R. Kavieff collection.)

Detroit Mafia captain Salvatore "Swinging Sammy" Serra is pictured attending a court proceeding in the late 1930s. Serra, who acquired his nickname due to his proficiency at using a baseball bat as an enforcement tool, was godfather Joe Zerilli's brother-in-law and a top lieutenant in the crime family throughout much of the middle half of the century. (Walter Reuther Library—Wayne State University.)

Onlookers and law enforcement congregate outside Boesky's Restaurant and Delicatessen, a popular Motor City eatery, as it looked on November 25, 1937, the night notorious Purple Gang enforcer Harry Millman was murdered inside. Feuding with the local Italian underworld, Millman was gunned down as he drank at the bar by East Coast assassins sent to kill him on orders from the Detroit Mafia. (Walter Reuther Library—Wayne State University.)

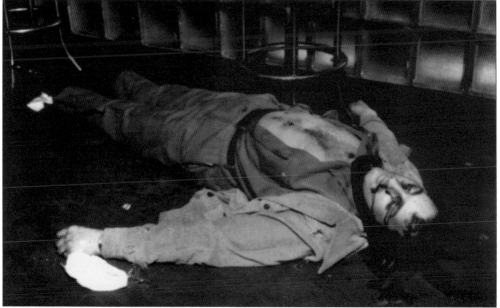

This crime scene photograph is of Millman, lying dead in a pool of his own blood on the floor, after being killed at the hands of hit men sent by local Italian Mafia powers Pete Licavoli and Joe Scarface Bommarito, carrying out a murder contract that was approved by Purple boss Abe Bernstein. After previous attempts to kill Millman had failed, Licavoli contracted the hit out to members of the New York underworld. (Paul R. Kaveiff collection.)

New York Mob hit man Harry "Happy" Maione is pictured in a New York Police Department mug shot from the 1930s. Maione, who was a member of the East Coast's notorious Mafia enforcement unit, Murder, Inc., came to Detroit in 1937 on orders from his underworld superiors to carry out the murder contract on Harry Millman. (Municipal archives of New York City.)

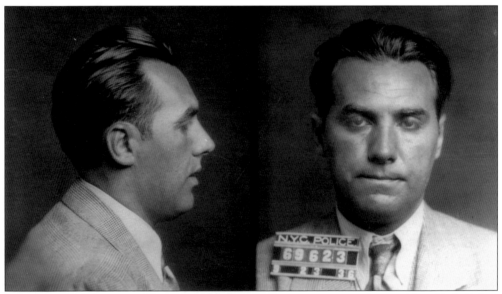

New York Mob hit man Harry "Pittsburg Phil" Strauss is pictured in a New York Police Department mug shot from the 1930s. Also a member of the infamous Murder, Inc., Strauss was dispatched to the Motor City, along with fellow underworld assassin Happy Maione, to execute Millman, who had gone too far in his feud with the Detroit Mafia. (Municipal archives of New York City.)

Detroit crime family soldier and notorious gangland strong-arm Matthew "Mike the Enforcer" Rubino is pictured during a court proceeding in the 1930s. Coming from a long line of local Mafia button men, his father and brother were both murdered in the city's early street wars, Rubino was one of the most-feared extortionists, debt collectors, and hit men in the area and a suspect in the 1930 shooting of Detroit police officer Henry Garven. He died in 1972. (Paul R. Kavieff collection)

Detroit Mob captain Salvatore "Sammy Lou" Lucido is pictured while waiting for a court appearance to begin in 1948. Lucido, who got his start in the River Gang, was the crime family's top gambling lieutenant for much of the second half of the century. Dying of cancer in 1985, Lucido passed on his large-scale bookmaking operation to his son and two nephews. (Walter Reuther Library—Wayne State University.)

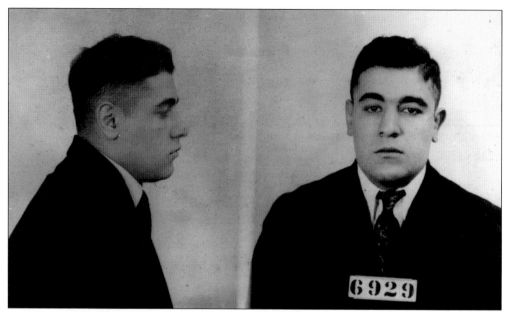

Local underworld figure Eddie Sarkesian is pictured in a DPD mug shot from the late 1930s. Found dead in his car in 1944, it is suspected Sarkesian began freelancing in the Motor City extortion rackets and was killed for his indiscretion by the Detroit Mafia. (Paul R. Kavieff collection.)

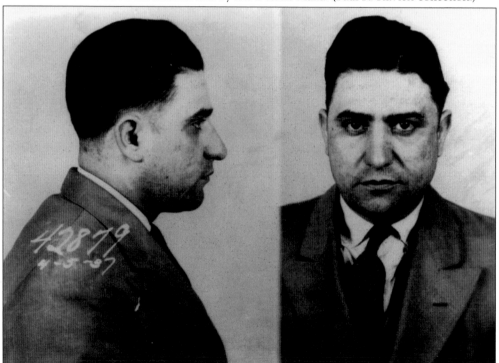

This DPD mug shot of area street tough Chris Scroy was taken after an arrest in the mid-1940s. Scroy, whose brother and cousin were murdered by the local crime syndicate in 1948, was killed by the Detroit Mafia in 1959 for shooting valued Mob lieutenant Max Stern almost a decade earlier. (Paul R. Kavieff collection.)

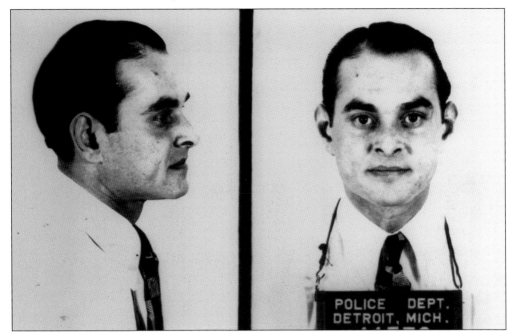

Former Purple Gang lieutenant Myron "Young Mikey" Selik is pictured in a DPD mug shot from 1948. Along with Harry Millman, Selik headed the Junior Purples and after Prohibition continued on in the Detroit underworld working for the Italians. Selik, who died in 1996, and Harry Ketwell, who died in 1997, were the last of the core Purple Gangers to pass away. (Paul R. Kavieff collection.)

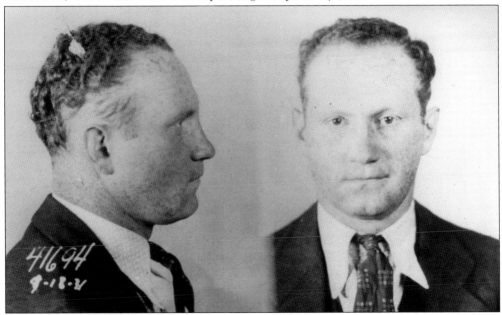

Teamsters Union power and former Purple Gang associate Paul "Red" Dorfman is shown in a DPD mug shot from the early 1930s. Placed in charge of the union's robust pension fund, Dorfman approved the first batch of an eventual multitude of pension fund loans to Mob-backed companies in order to finance the Mafia's investment in Las Vegas. His son Allen followed him into labor politics and was killed by the Mob in 1983. (Paul R. Kavieff collection.)

Detroit Mob lieutenant Paul Vitale is pictured in an FBI mug shot from the early 1970s. Controlling all the vice in the city's highly popular Greektown district, Vitale was a major player in the area's sanitation industry and married both of his daughters to the sons of powerful Motor City wiseguy Pete Corrado. Vitale died in 1990, while living in semi-retirement in Mount Clemens, Michigan. (Author's collection.)

Area Mafia chief Peter "Bozzi" Vitale, the younger and more infamous brother to local Mob captain Paul Vitale, is shown as he leaves court in the mid-1960s. Alongside his brother, Bozzi lead the crime family's migration into the city's sanitation industry and, in 1962, married off his youngest daughter to Joseph Barbara Jr., the son of New York Mafia lieutenant Joseph "Joe the Barber" Barbara Sr. Vitale, eventually named a captain in the crime family himself in the early 1970s, died of natural causes in 1997. (Walter Reuther Library—Wayne State University.)

Four

THE ZERILLI ERA

Following five years at the helm of the local underworld and solidifying a legacy that will be remembered for the seemingly effortless and tremendously profitable transition of the Detroit crime family into the post-Prohibition era, Black Bill Tocco, the city's first La Cosa Nostra don, was sent to prison for tax evasion. Leaving the Motor City for federal incarceration in the latter part of 1936, Tocco tapped his brother-in-law and underboss, Joe Zerilli, to be his successor. Taking the reins of the area's gangland syndicate at the age of 39, Zerilli would go on to head the Detroit Mob for over 40 years, building the crime family into a juggernaut of vice and corruption and a model of underworld stability and efficiency. Zerilli was so well respected by his peers he was given a seat on "the Commission," the U.S. Mafia's supreme governing council and an honor bestowed upon very few godfathers outside of New York City.

Throughout his tenure as don, Joe Zerilli's true genius was exhibited by the beneficial ties he created for the crime family in the city's labor unions, as well as his very low-profile yet extremely successful takeover of the local drug networks. Add to that his highly profitable decision in the late 1940s to invade and take over the numerous illegal rackets being conducted in the area's African American community, the crown jewel of which was the black-market numbers lottery, and the Mob's infiltration of the Las Vegas gaming industry, and Zerilli took the Detroit Mafia to astronomic heights of power. Insulating himself through an intricate maze of emissaries, lieutenants, and shell companies, the Midwest godfather oversaw his vast and expansive criminal empire virtually unscathed from government intrusion, encouraging intermarriage among his soldiers families as a means of maintaining maximum loyalty within the ranks of his crime family. Naming Angelo Meli his underboss, Giovanni "Papa John" Priziola his consiglieri, and Anthony "Tony Jack" Giacalone the syndicate's street boss, Zerilli ruled the Motor City from 1936 until his death in 1977, never serving any significant time behind bars.

Motor City Mafia power Pietro "Machine Gun Pete" Corrado is shown as he leaves court in the mid-1950s. Getting his start in the local underworld as a gunman for the River Gang, Corrado, also known as "Pete the Enforcer," was Joe Zerilli's brother-in-law and was named a captain in the Detroit crime family in the 1930s. In the next decade, Zerilli tapped Corrado to spur the syndicate's takeover of the city's numbers racket, a job he maintained until his death from a heart attack in 1957. (Walter Reuther Library—Wayne State University.)

This late-1960s FBI mug shot is of Dominic "Sparky" Corrado, younger brother of area Mob heavyweight Pietro Corrado. A local strong-arm and hit man, as well as a top member of his brother's crew, Sparky died of natural causes in 1976 at the age of 62. (Walter Reuther Library—Wayne State University.)

Detroit Mob lieutenant Dominic "Fats" Corrado, oldest son of former Motor City Mafia captain Pietro Corrado, is pictured as he leaves court in the 1970s. Following his father's death in 1957, Fats was selected to take over his crew, as well as the area's profitable illegal numbers lottery. (Walter Reuther Library—Wayne State University.)

Infamous Motor City crime family figure Anthony "Tony the Bull" Corrado (seated left), youngest son of former Detroit Mob captain Pietro Corrado, is pictured while meeting with his attorneys in the late 1950s. Heading the syndicate's enforcement wing, Tony the Bull took over as captain of his older brother Fats's crew in 1985 following his death of a heart attack. (Walter Reuther Library—Wayne State University.)

The inside of the former popular Detroit area restaurant the Grecian Gardens, located on Grand Boulevard and Monroe Avenue and owned and operated by the notorious Corrado family, is shown as it looked on a busy Saturday evening in the mid-1960s. The eatery was also a place where younger members of the crime family would get their start working as hosts, coat checks, and waiters, using the connections they made there to springboard to future advancement in the syndicate hierarchy. (Walter Reuther Library—Wayne State University.)

Former Motor City Mafia overlord Black Bill Tocco is shown while answering questions before the Kefauver committee. Tocco, who had been living in Florida since his release from prison in the mid-1940s, was called back to Detroit in 1951 to testify in front of the committee about his role in the area's organized crime syndicate. Dying in 1972, Tocco spent his final years in semi-retirement in Miami, offering counsel to his associates in the Midwest from afar. (Walter Reuther Library—Wayne State University.)

Detroit crime family soldier Paul Tocco is pictured being booked at the DPD on gambling charges in the 1940s. Tocco, whose father was slain Motor City underworld power Joe Tocco and whose uncle was former area Mafia don Bill Tocco, married the daughter of local Mob boss Joe Zerilli. (Walter Reuther Library—Wayne State University.)

Local gangland figure Louis "Rip" Koury is pictured entering the federal courthouse in the 1960s. One of the city's top racketeers and the area's largest independent numbers kingpin, Koury, who was Lebanese, had close ties to the Detroit Mafia and in the 1970s, was assigned to head the crime family's infiltration of all rackets being conducted in suburban Pontiac, Michigan, a primarily black community and a hotbed of illegal activity. (Walter Reuther Library—Wayne State University.)

Detroit Mafia powerhouse Onofrio "Nono" Minaudo is pictured in the mid-1950s speaking with reporters. Minaudo, who along with Joseph "Cockeyed Joe" Catalanotte was responsible for looking after the crime family's interests in Canada, owned numerous local bowling alleys and several area vending machine companies. Minaudo was killed in 1965 while in Sicily. (Walter Reuther Library—Wayne State University.)

Motor City Mob captain and former bootlegging czar Pete Licavoli is shown while leaving for federal prison in the 1950s. Following Bill Tocco's imprisonment in 1936, newly-christened godfather Joe Zerilli placed Licavoli in charge of the crime family's financial affairs, as well as all the syndicate's out-of-state underworld interests. Retiring to his ranch in Arizona in the latter years of his life, Licavoli died there of a heart attack in 1984. (Walter Reuther Library—Wayne State University.)

Future Cleveland Mafia boss James "Blackie" Licavoli is pictured while testifying at the Kefauver hearings in 1951. Known on the streets as "Jack White," Licavoli was a former River Gang member and first cousin to Detroit Mob lieutenant Pete Licavoli, who moved to Ohio after Prohibition and became the Cleveland crime family's representative in Youngstown. In 1976, Licavoli was named to succeed longtime Midwest godfather John Scalish as don of the Cleveland Mafia. Engaging in a lengthy street war with underworld rivals, Licavoli was jailed in 1982 for his role in the bloody feud and soon thereafter became the nation's first Mob boss ever convicted under the highly influential Racketeer Influenced and Corrupt Organizations (RICO) statute. (Walter Reuther Library—Wayne State University.)

This is a picture of a mid-1950s DPD Board of Inquiry, which convened to investigate Mafia activity in the city. Notice Vincent Piersante (second from right), who at the time of this photograph was head of the department's organized crime squad and through the years undoubtedly became the Motor City crime family's biggest adversary in local law enforcement. (Walter Reuther Library—Wayne State University.)

Detroit Mafia gambling lieutenant Max Stern is shown as he leaves a court appearance in the mid-1950s. At the height of his power, Stern, known by friends and associates as "Big Maxie," was the most powerful Jewish wiseguy in the Motor City, working closely under area gangland titan Pete Licavoli. Stern died of natural causes in 1972. (Walter Reuther Library—Wayne State University.)

Anthony "Tony Z" Zerilli (left), alongside gangland associate and first cousin Anthony "Tony T" Tocco (right), is shown as the pair of Detroit Mob royalty pose for a snapshot at a local social function in the early 1950s. Tony Z, area godfather Joe Zerilli's son, who had been initiated or "made" into the Motor City crime family in 1949, was on the rise to great power in the Detroit underworld due to his bloodline, while Tony T, former don Bill Tocco's son, who became a made member of the local Mafia in the 1950s, garnered headlines for his high-profile marriage to the daughter of East Coast Mob boss Joe Profaci. Zerilli, who also married one of Profaci's daughters, would go on to become the syndicate's underboss, and Tocco its consiglieri. (Walter Reuther Library—Wayne State University.)

Detroit crime family soldier Caesar Badalamenti is pictured in an FBI surveillance photograph from the late 1960s. Badalamenti, whose uncle was former gangland boss John Vitale, was a top lieutenant in the area drug market and acted as the local Mafia's liaison to the Sicilian underworld. (Author's collection.)

Local Mob power Anthony D'Anna is shown in a professional photograph taken in the early 1970s. An early member of the city's Mafia family, D'Anna made a name for himself in 1938 by allegedly ordering the killing of area crime lord Joe Tocco. D'Anna went on to become the syndicate's representative to the area's automobile industry, maintaining very close ties to the Ford Motor Company. He died in 1984. (Author's collection.)

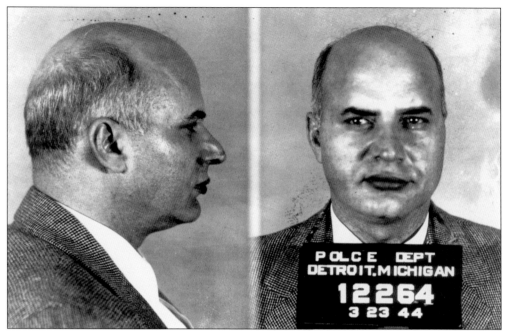

Motor City Mafia chief Angelo Meli is pictured in a DPD mug shot from the 1940s. A leader of the local underworld during Prohibition, Meli was tapped to be the inaugural Detroit crime family's consiglieri and then its underboss, eventually spearheading the Motor City Mob's infiltration of the labor unions. Meli died of heart failure in 1969. (Paul R. Kaveiff collection.)

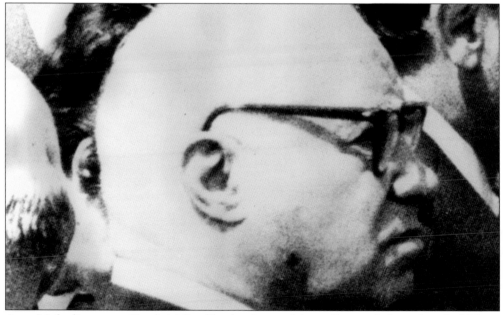

Area Mafia lieutenant Frank Meli, older brother to Motor City underboss Angelo Meli, is pictured in an FBI surveillance photograph from the late 1960s. Meli made his mark in the area's underworld by dominating the Motor City extortion and vending machine rackets, as well as aiding his younger sibling in managing the syndicate's labor affairs. Meli died in 1988 in Sterling Heights. (Author's collection.)

Motor City Mob icon Anthony "Tony Jack" Giacalone is shown in an FBI surveillance photograph from the early 1970s. Undoubtedly the most well-recognized Detroit underworld figure of the 20th century, Giacalone got his start as a driver and bodyguard for local Mafia don Joe Zerilli and was soon made a captain in the crime family. In the late 1960s, he was named street boss over the entire syndicate and the Mob's liaison to labor power Jimmy Hoffa. (Author's collection.)

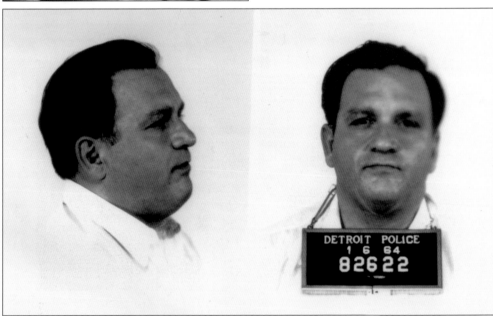

Detroit Mafia lieutenant Vito "Billy Jack" Giacalone is pictured in a DPD mug shot taken in 1964. Younger brother of local Mob kingpin Tony Jack and known as a diligent street earner, Billy Jack served as one of the crime family's top bookmakers and loan sharks until he was named a captain in the late 1960s and given authority over his own crew. Giacalone also oversaw syndicate activity in Toledo, primarily delegating authority through his top lieutenant in Ohio, Anthony "Whitey" Beasase. (Paul R. Kavieff collection.)

Detroit underworld figure Carlo Licata is shown in an FBI surveillance photograph taken in the early 1970s. Initiated into the California Mafia in the 1950s by his father and former Detroiter Nick Licata, the reigning Mob don of Los Angeles, Carlo moved to the area upon marrying Motor City godfather Bill Tocco's daughter. Licata's former home in Bloomfield Hills is believed by authorities to have been the site of Jimmy Hoffa's execution on July 30, 1975. Six years to the date of the high-profile labor leader's disappearance/murder, on July 30, 1981, Licata was found dead at the same residence, under suspicious circumstances. Until now, this theory on Hoffa's murder had never been made public. (Author's collection.)

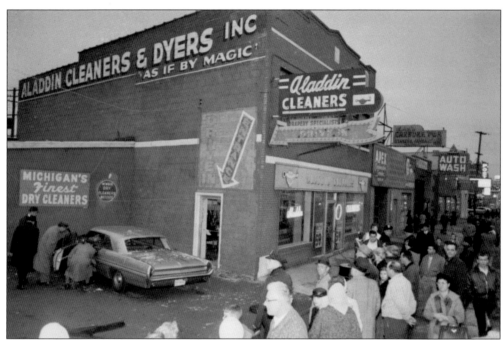

Motor City Mob captain Santo "Cockeyed Sam" Perrone (below) testifies before the Kefauver committee in 1951. Cutting his teeth in the local underworld as a highly feared gunman for the River Gang, Perrone, also known as "Sammy the Shark," achieved great power in the Detroit Mafia, becoming one of the city's biggest labor racketeers and black-market extortionists. In the early 1960s, Perrone and a crew of grizzled Mob veterans went to war with a faction of the crime family's younger generation, in particular, up-and-coming gangland star Anthony "Tony Jack" Giacalone, and ended up getting his leg blown off in a car explosion meant to kill him (above). Perrone died in 1973 of natural causes, while Giacalone continued his meteoric rise through the local Mob hierarchy. (Walter Reuther Library—Wayne State University.)

Detroit crime family member Salvatore "Sammy B" Bagnasco is shown in an FBI surveillance photograph taken in the early 1970s. A close confidant to local Mob boss Joe Zerilli and his family, Bagnasco owned and operated Bagnasco's Funeral Home in Gross Pointe. Authorities believe the funeral home was used by the area Mafia to hold secret meetings, as well as a possible location that was used to cremate Jimmy Hoffa's dead body. (Author's collection.)

Area Mob leader Dominic Bommarito is pictured in an FBI surveillance photograph from the early 1970s. Bommarito, who comes from a long line of Detroit Mafia royalty, was a well-respected and heavily feared lieutenant in the local underworld. (Author's collection.)

Motor City Mafia gambling lieutenant Sol Shindel stands in court in 1971. One of the most powerful Jewish wiseguys in the area, Shindel ran a highly profitable bookmaking operation out of the Anchor Bar, located in downtown Detroit. Shindel was killed in his home on December 6, 1971, after both he and several members of the city's crime family were indicted for their role in the illegal gambling operation. (Walter Reuther Library—Wayne State University.)

Detroit underworld enforcer Pete Vasallo is shown in a DPD mug shot from the late 1950s. A longtime strong-arm in the Motor City Mafia, Vasallo was murdered in 1972, three years after taking part in the unauthorized beating death of Sam Di Maggio, a local wiseguy in gambling debt to the area Mob syndicate. (Walter Reuther Library—Wayne State University.)

Hollywood actor and former Detroit Lions All-Pro defensive lineman Alex Karas, and his first wife, Joan, are pictured here in a newspaper photograph from 1969. A league investigation into Karas's heavily rumored off-the-field behavior revealed his involvement in rampant sports wagering and ties to the notorious Giacalone brothers and the city's organized crime family, as well as widespread gambling activity taking place at the Lindell AC, a popular downtown bar he co-owned. After the NFL inquiry was completed, commissioner Pete Rozelle suspended Karas for the entire 1963 professional football season. (Above, Walter Reuther Library—Wayne State University; below, author's collection.)

Motor City Mob chief Michael "Big Mike" Polizzi is shown in an FBI surveillance photograph from the 1970s. Polizzi, whose father-in-law was syndicate superpower Giovanni "Papa John" Priziola, was assigned to lead the crime family's foray into Las Vegas and was eventually named the local Mafia's consiglieri. Demoted from the post due to his son Angelo's decision to cooperate with the government, Polizzi died in 1997 estranged from his former associates in the Mob. (Author's collection.)

Detroit Mafia captain Rafaelle "Jimmy Q" Quassarano is pictured in an FBI surveillance photograph from the mid-1970s. One of the crime family's primary narcotic lieutenants, Quassarano made his headquarters at Motor City Barber and Beauty Supply and married the daughter of Sicilian Mob lord Vittorio "Don Vito" Vitale. Briefly appointed consiglieri in the late 1970s, Quassarano was forced to relinquish the highly-valued leadership position when he was sent to prison in 1981. (Author's collection.)

Longtime Motor City Mob lieutenant Salvatore "Sam Jacobs" Finazzo is shown in an FBI surveillance photograph taken in the mid-1970s. Brother-in-law of godfather Joe Zerilli, Finazzo got his start during Prohibition as a strong-arm in the East Side Gang and was eventually named a captain in the local crime family. Finazzo died in 1994 after heading the syndicate's interests in the area's boxing community for many years. (Author's collection.)

Former Detroit Tigers All-Star hurler Denny McClain (middle) is pictured posing for a publicity photograph in 1966 with fellow starting pitchers Mickey Lolich and Joe Sparma. According to underworld lore, McClain's foot injury, which forced him to miss time at the tail end of the 1967 pennant race, was allegedly caused by a member of the local Mafia who stomped on his toe over a dispute regarding his unpaid gambling debts. (Walter Reuther Library—Wayne State University.)

Motor City crime family soldier Joseph Barbara Jr. is pictured in an FBI surveillance photograph from the 1960s. Barbara, whose father, Buffalo Mafia captain Joseph "Joe the Barber" Barbara Sr., hosted the infamous 1957 mega-Mob conference in Apalachin, New York, came to Detroit in the late 1950s after marrying the daughter of local gangland figure Peter "Bozzi" Vitale. (Author's collection.)

Longtime Detroit Mafia attorney William Buffalino is pictured speaking to reporters in a press photograph from the 1970s. Developing an impeccable reputation as the premiere defense lawyer to the area's Mob syndicate, Buffalino was a first cousin to Pennsylvania crime boss Russell Buffalino, who is one of those suspected of sanctioning the Jimmy Hoffa murder. (Author's collection.)

Five

HOFFA

Born on February 14, 1913, in Brazil, Indiana, James R. (Jimmy) Hoffa came to Detroit with his family in the early 1920s and quickly became an important figure in the city's vast and highly populated labor community. The diminutive yet ferocious Midwestern truck driver made a name for himself in 1931, when he organized a strike of all the workers in the city who made a living unloading boxes of produce off trucks at Detroit's Kroger Grocery and Baking Company. On the fast track to power in big-time labor politics, Hoffa joined the International Brotherhood of Teamsters—a union primarily devoted to the welfare of workers in the trucking industry—and helped turn it into the most dominant labor union in the entire country, becoming its vice president in 1952 and its president in 1957.

A great deal of Hoffa's power base came from his close relationship with several influential members of the Mafia; they provided him with muscle, protection, and job security and in return, he gave them unlimited access to the union's stout pension fund, which they used to finance their investment in several enormously profitable Las Vegas hotels and casinos. Jailed in 1967 on federal criminal charges of bribery and jury tampering, Hoffa was forced to step down from the Teamsters's presidency and hand the top spot in the union to his vice president, Frank Fitzsimmons. Emerging from prison in 1972 and unable to wrestle control of the union back from Fitzsimmons and his Mob backers, Hoffa allegedly threatened several key mafioso, telling them he would reveal the relationship between the Teamsters and La Cosa Nostra if they did not place him back in the presidency. Unwilling to negotiate with Hoffa, it is believed the Mafia placed a contract on his life. Jimmy Hoffa disappeared on July 30, 1975, and was last seen in a suburban Detroit restaurant parking lot congregating with unidentified men in a car. Hoffa's body has never been found, and he was declared legally dead in 1983; however, the shroud of mystery and suspicion surrounding his death to this day makes it the most notorious unsolved crime in U.S. history.

Jimmy Hoffa (far left) is pictured as a child in a photograph taken with his four siblings on his family's farm in Brazil, Indiana. Moving with his family to Detroit in the early 1920s in order for his father to find employment in the city's fledgling automobile industry, Hoffa eventually began his work in the area's labor community by spending several years unloading produce trucks full of strawberries at the Kroger Grocery and Baking Company. (Walter Reuther Library—Wayne State University.)

Hoffa, upon entering the second chapter of his life in the labor workforce, is pictured behind the wheel of his truck. After organizing a strike of all the workers who unloaded produce cargo at the Kroger warehouse dock in protest of unfair wages, Hoffa was fired and took a job as a truck driver for a local hauling company. (Walter Reuther Library—Wayne State University.)

Hoffa, pictured as a young man, plays dice on a local street corner with his friends. Following his time hauling freight across the country, the eager and ambitious Hoffa began recruiting and organizing trucking employees for the International Brotherhood of Teamsters, a labor union devoted to the health, interests, and welfare of the American trucker. (Walter Reuther Library—Wayne State University.)

On the heels of an unprecedented rise through the ranks of the Teamsters, Hoffa became the youngest person ever elected to the union's administrative council and in 1952, became its vice president. Hoffa assumed the powerful union's top seat when Teamsters president Dave Beck, pictured here with Hoffa in a 1950s press photograph, was indicted and jailed on federal bribery charges in 1957. (Walter Reuther Library—Wayne State University.)

Pictured in 1965, alongside his vice president and top lieutenant, Frank Fitzsimmons, at a rally for striking truck drivers that took place at Cobo Hall, the beloved union boss speaks to a large crowd of disgruntled labor workers. Hoffa and Fitzsimmons would soon become bitter enemies, engaging in a highly volatile feud and heavily layered dispute that ended up with Fitzsimmons's son's car being blown up and Hoffa being killed. (Walter Reuther Library—Wayne State University.)

Teamsters Union Local 299, pictured above and located on Trumble Avenue, two blocks north of Tiger Stadium, was Jimmy Hoffa's power base in the city of Detroit. From his position in the Teamsters presidency, Hoffa appointed several key allies to top positions at the Motor City local union hall. (Authors collection.)

Following convictions on federal charges of bribery and jury tampering in 1966, Hoffa, pictured here in the backseat of the car transporting him to Lewisburg Federal Penitentiary in Pennsylvania, exhausted all appellate options before finally being incarcerated in 1967. While in jail, Hoffa was succeeded in the union presidency by Frank Fitzsimmons. Due to his relationship with several top mobsters, Hoffa was afforded special treatment at Lewisburg, residing in a wing of the prison called Mafia Manor. (Walter Reuther Library—Wayne State University.)

Shown here is the parking lot of Nemo's Bar, a popular downtown area watering hole and the site of the July 1975 bombing of local union vice president Richard "Little Fitz" Fitzsimmons's car in a suspected attempt by Hoffa to take the lives of both Fitzsimmons and his father, Frank. After being rebuffed in his attempts to reenter union politics by Frank Fitzsimmons and then the Mafia, Hoffa declared war on both. (Author's collection.)

Hoffa, in January 1972 at Metropolitan Airport, is flanked by his lawyer and wife as he makes his return home to the Motor City after being released from the prison on a presidential pardon arranged by Frank Fitzsimmons, Hoffa's successor in the Teamster's political hierarchy, and granted to him by Richard M. Nixon. Following several extravagant welcome-home parties held in the area in the weeks after his return, Hoffa immediately set out to reclaim his post as the Teamsters Union president. To Hoffa's great dismay, he soon found out that Fitzsimmons, with encouragement from his Mob superiors, had agreed to a stipulation in the pardon that barred his return to labor politics. (Walter Reuther Library—Wayne State University.)

Here is the site of the Machus Red Fox Restaurant, in Bloomfield Township, Michigan, as it looked on the day Jimmy Hoffa disappeared on July 30, 1975. Today it stands as the popular Italian eatery Andiamo. The restaurant's parking lot was the last place Jimmy Hoffa was ever seen alive. Scheduled to meet with power-wielding crime lords Anthony "Tony Jack" Giacalone and Anthony "Tony Pro" Provenzano at 2:30 p.m. in order to discuss gaining support for his bid to recapture the Teamsters' presidency, Hoffa was stood-up and called his wife from a nearby hardware store pay phone to tell her he was coming home. Walking back to his car, witnesses saw Hoffa approached by an automobile with several unidentified men in it. Shortly thereafter, the witnesses saw Hoffa get in the backseat of the unidentified automobile and drive away, never to be seen or heard from again. (Walter Reuther Library—Wayne State University.)

Detroit crime family soldier Joseph "Joey Jack" Giacalone (right) is pictured talking to an associate in an FBI surveillance photograph from the 1980s. Son of area Mob legend Anthony "Tony Jack" Giacalone, Joey and his brother Anthony "Fat Tony" Giacalone Jr. lead much of the area Mafia's investment in the local construction industry. The young Giacalone's 1975 maroon Lincoln Mercury sedan was seized by the government following Hoffa's disappearance, believed to be driven by Charles "Chuckie" O'Brein—Hoffa's surrogate son—on the afternoon the labor czar was murdered. Federal authorities believe the vehicle was used to transport Hoffa from the Red Fox parking lot to the location where he was killed. In recent years, the FBI has matched a hair found in the backseat of the automobile to a hair taken from one of Hoffa's old hairbrushes. (Above, Wayne State University; left, author's collection.)

The Andretta brothers, Thomas (center) and Stephen (left), New Jersey–area Teamsters and associates of East Coast Mafia chief Anthony "Tony Pro" Provenzano as well as alleged coconspirators in the Hoffa hit, are pictured together on August 21, 1975, after their testimony before a federal grand jury investigating the labor leader's disappearance. Never charged with any crimes relating to the Hoffa murder, both brothers were incarcerated soon thereafter on unrelated convictions. (Walter Reuther Library—Wayne State University.)

In a book released in 2004, former Hoffa ally and Mob strong-arm Francis "Frank the Irishman" Sheerhan alleges that this residence, located off 7 Mile Road in Northwest Detroit, was the house used to assassinate the beleaguered labor leader. Authorities on the investigation discredit the now-dead Sheerhan's account. (Author's collection.)

This house in Bloomfield Hills, formerly owned by Detroit Mafia lieutenant Carlo Licata and his wife, area Mob boss Jack Tocco's sister, is believed by many authorities in the investigation to be the location that Hoffa was taken to and murdered after leaving the Machus Red Fox, a mere two-minute drive from the parking lot where he was last seen alive. The FBI speculates that Provenzano lieutenants Salvatore "Sally Buggs" Briguglio and the Andrettas, as well as, most likely, a representative from the Detroit crime family performed the hit. (Author's collection.)

The Hidden Dreams Ranch is pictured here in May 2006, as FBI agents dig for remains of Jimmy Hoffa on a parcel of farm property in Milford, formerly owned by Hoffa associate Roland McMaster. Investigators called the lead, acquired via a tip from an imprisoned McMaster confidant, the biggest break in the case in over 20 years. After two weeks of digging, the FBI called off the search, having not found anything of significance. (Author's collection.)

Six

PASSING OF THE TORCH

In April 1977, longtime Detroit godfather Joe Zerilli died of heart failure. His death concluded a storied chapter in the history of the Motor City underworld and began another. Just over two years later, on June 11, 1979, Zerilli's nephew and gangland protégé Giacomo "Black Jack" Tocco, the son of former city Mob don Black Bill Tocco, was officially installed as boss of the Detroit Mafia at a top-secret inauguration ceremony held at the Timberland Farms Ranch located in Dexter, Michigan. A new era was dawning, and a new generation of wiseguys, mostly comprised of sons, nephews, and cousins of several top Zerilli lieutenants, were assuming the reins of the crime family and helping it transition into what was an increasingly changing Mafia landscape.

However, Jack Tocco's assent to power, perceived by many on the outside as smooth and without contention, was haggled by internal strife. Initially, when Joe Zerilli went into semi-retirement in the late 1960s, moving to Florida to live out his later years with his brother-in-law and gangland-counterpart Bill Tocco, he named his son Anthony "Tony Z" Zerilli acting boss of the crime family. But the elder Zerilli's days in the sun were short-lived, and he was called back to his post in Detroit in the early 1970s when Anthony was convicted and jailed for stealing over $6 million from the Frontier Hotel and Casino in Las Vegas. At this juncture, Joe Zerilli made a controversial decision and demoted his son from the boss's chair, tapping his nephew Jack Tocco as his new successor and heir apparent to the Motor City Mob throne. Tocco, in gesture of goodwill, named Anthony Zerilli his underboss, and the two cousins set fourth to take the Detroit Mafia into the last two decades of the century, a time where the syndicate's profile would become significantly lower, while its grip of power over the city's underworld would grow in the shadows.

Anthony Zerilli (center) is pictured in November 1977 alongside his wife and mother, leaving the funeral of his father, legendary Detroit godfather Joe Zerilli. Accompanied in this photograph by underworld associate Anthony Corrado (next to Zerilli on the right), the area's Mafia prince was ushered back to the Motor City by U.S. marshals to attend the funeral on a granted leave from serving time in federal prison. (Walter Reuther Library—Wayne State University.)

Longtime Motor City crime family consiglieri Giovanni "Papa John" Priziola is greeted by associates Anthony Corrado and Joseph "Joe the Whip" Triglia as the trio arrives to attend Zerilli's funeral. This FBI surveillance photograph of Priziola, the local Mob's top narcotic lieutenant, and its man placed in charge of overseeing all crime family interests on the West Coast, is one of the last ever taken of the longtime underworld chieftain. Following Zerilli's passing, Priziola became the syndicate's titular head before dying himself two years later in April 1979. (Author's collection.)

This FBI surveillance photograph shows several high-ranking members of the Detroit Mob syndicate and their wives and families leaving Joe Zerilli's wake held at Bagnasco's Funeral Home in Gross Pointe. Pay special attention to local Mafia superpowers Anthony Giacalone (No. 11), flanked by his two sons, Joe (No. 9) and Anthony Jr. (No. 10), and Jack Tocco (No. 2), accompanied by his wife, Marie (No. 3), son Vito (No. 7), and daughter-in-law Kim (No. 8). Also notice area gangland figures Salvatore Finazzo (No. 6), Ray Lanese (No. 13), Tony Ferlitto (No. 4), and Pat Carlini (No. 15), congregating at the event. The syndicate would wait almost two years to name an official successor. (Author's collection.)

Detroit Mafia don Giacomo "Black Jack" Tocco is shown in an FBI surveillance photograph taken in the late 1970s, just prior to his taking over as boss of the Zerilli crime family. Tocco, who made his headquarters at Melrose Linen Service and is married to former underboss Angelo Meli's daughter, was officially installed as the syndicate's godfather in July 1979 at a top-secret inauguration ceremony 45 miles outside the city, in Dexter, Michigan. (Author's collection.)

Anthony Zerilli is shown in an FBI mug shot taken in the late 1970s. Originally tapped as his father's successor, Zerilli was convicted and sent to prison for his role in stealing money from the Frontier Hotel and Casino in Las Vegas. As a result of his incarceration, he was demoted from his position as acting boss and replaced by his cousin Jack Tocco. (Author's collection.)

Anthony Tocco, younger brother to Motor City Mob boss Jack Tocco, is pictured dispensing orders to an underworld associate in an early 1980s FBI surveillance photograph. Highly respected within the Detroit crime family, Tocco served as a captain in the 1970s and 1980s before being named consiglieri by his brother in the 1990s, a role he still maintains today. (Author's collection.)

Motor City crime lord Vincent "Little Vince" Meli is shown in an FBI surveillance photograph taken while attending Joe Zerilli's funeral in 1977. Nephew of former Mafia underboss Angelo Meli, Vince graduated from Notre Dame in 1942 and served in World War II before joining his uncle within the ranks of the area crime family. Meli is currently one of the highest-ranking members in the Detroit Mob hierarchy. (Author's collection.)

Anthony Corrado is pictured walking the city streets while making his daily collections in the late 1970s. This photograph taken by federal agents from over 100 yards away shows how sophisticated, even at that time, the government's surveillance techniques were and how easily local underworld figures can be watched. (Author's collection.)

Local underworld strong-arm Jack "Jackie G" Gianosa (right) is pictured in an FBI surveillance photograph from the mid-1970s. A first cousin to underboss Tony Zerilli and a grandson to former don Joe Zerilli, Gianosa acted as the Zerilli crew's top street emissary, delivering messages, providing muscle, and overseeing the day-to-day operations of various crew rackets. (Author's collection.)

Jack Gianosa is pictured with an associate, standing outside Anthony Zerilli's business office in Roseville, Michigan, in an FBI surveillance photograph. Area Mafia prince Zerilli owned several legitimate local companies, Bella Mia Pasta and Sauce Company and the Spaghetti Palace, a popular local eatery, among them. Gianosa ran the Spaghetti Palace on behalf of his cousin; the location acted as the Zerilli crew headquarters. (Author's collection.)

Widely feared Motor City gangland enforcer Thomas "Tommy Gun" Lewis is pictured in a 1976 FBI mug shot. One of the local Mafia's most often utilized strong-arms, Lewis worked directly under crime family captain Dominic "Fats" Corrado, collecting underworld debts and extorting Mob street taxes from area businesses and vice peddlers. (Author's collection.)

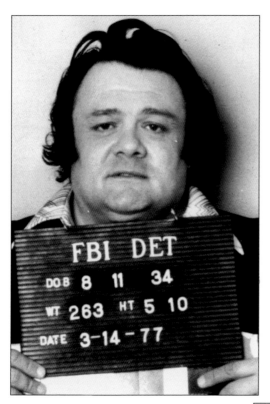

Longtime Detroit Mafia captain Antonio "T. R." Ruggirello Jr. is seen in an FBI mug shot taken in the late 1970s. Son of the late Antonio "Tony" Ruggirello Sr., a former top button man in the local crime syndicate, T. R. co-owned an area pest extermination company with Tony Giacalone and was a close ally to Mob boss Jack Tocco. (Author's collection.)

Area Mob soldier Luigi "Louie the Bulldog" Ruggirello is pictured in a DPD mug shot from the 1960s. A sibling of local Mafia heavy T. R. Ruggirello, Luigi and his brother co-owned Timberland Farms Game Ranch (located in Dexter, Michigan) an upscale hunting lodge where in July 1979, Jack Tocco was officially elected don of the Motor City Mafia. (Author's collection.)

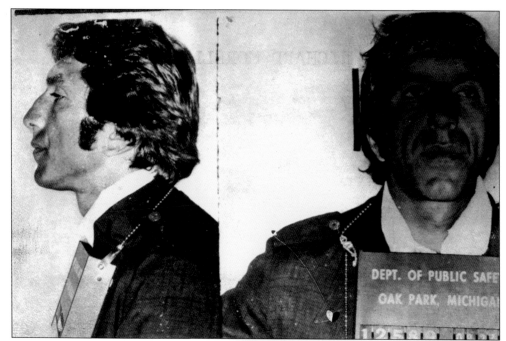

Local Mafia enforcer Ronald "Hollywood Ronnie" Morelli is pictured in an early 1970s police mug shot (above) and in an FBI surveillance photograph (right) showing him leaving court in June 1971 following an arraignment on bookmaking charges. Morelli's codefendant in the 1971 case was Detroit crime family gambling chief Sol Shindel, who, six months later, was found dead in his suburban Southfield residence, shot in the face. Being groomed for a future leadership role in the Motor City Mob hierarchy, Morelli, who got his nickname due to his flashy demeanor and playboy lifestyle, was sent to jail in the early 1980s and subsequently died there in 1985 of a massive heart attack while playing a game of racquetball. Until his death Morelli remained the top suspect in the Shindel homicide. (Author's collection.)

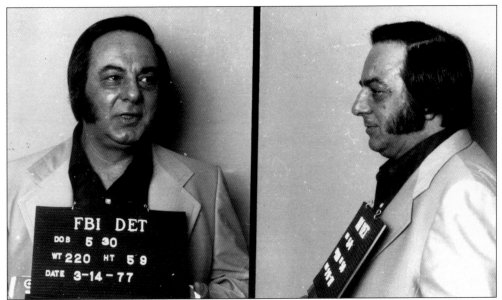

Detroit Mob soldier Peter "Pete the Baker" Cavataio is pictured in a 1970s FBI mug shot. Cavataio, who along with his two brothers, Dominic and Julian, also area Mafia lieutenants, owned several city bakeries, married the daughter of former crime family powerhouse Pete Corrado. Killed in 1985 after accruing major gambling debts to various local underworld figures, Cavataio remains the last made member of the Motor City Mafia to be murdered. (Author's collection.)

Motor City crime family soldier Anthony "Tony Pal" Palazzola is pictured leaving an area supermarket in a mid-1970s FBI surveillance photograph. Palazzola, whose father, Salvatore "Sammy Pal" Palazzola, was also a member of the local Mafia, was appointed Detroit gangland representative to Canada in the early 1980s, replacing Sam Caruso and Nick Cicchini. (Author's collection.)

This FBI photograph is of a dead fish, which was sent by the Detroit Mafia to a local bar owner through the mail, in an attempt to warn the tavern's proprietor that if he continued to refuse to pay tribute money, he would soon be "sleeping with the fishes"—an underworld ploy adopted straight from the Hollywood motion picture *The Godfather*. In most major cities, Detroit included, all bars and restaurants operating within designated Mob territory are required to cut the local crime family in for a percentage of their total weekly profits (a term referred to in Mafia circles as "tribute"), an extortion racket long employed by gangland administrations. (Author's collection.)

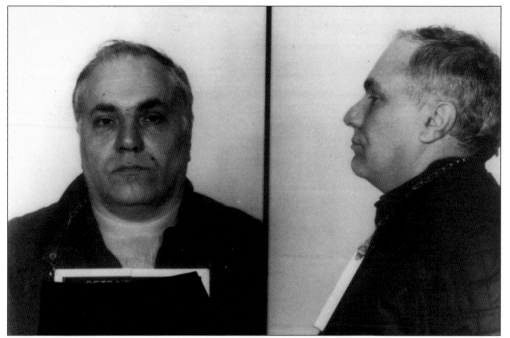

Detroit Mob figure Frank "Frankie the Bomb" Bommarito is pictured in an early-1980s FBI mug shot. At the time this picture was taken, Bommarito was a loan shark, extortionist, and top strong-arm for the Giaccalone crew. A descendent of local Mafia royalty, Bommarito was also the crime family's man in charge of relations with the area motorcycle gangs. (Author's collection.)

Detroit biker gang kingpin Harry "Taco" Bowman is pictured in an FBI mug shot from the late 1970s. Leader of the Outlaws, a fearsome nationwide motorcycle gang and a viciously lethal crime syndicate within their own right, Bowman and his associates worked closely with the local Mafia, often being used for muscle work and drug distribution. Currently serving a lifetime prison sentence, in his final years on the street Bowman had a falling out with the Mob and had a murder contract put on his head. (Author's collection.)

Several members of the Detroit crime family and one of their attorneys congregate outside the Joe Zerilli funeral. Pictured from left to right are Tony Corrado, Tony Tocco, Jack Tocco, Rafealle Quassarano, attorney Peter Bellanca, and Dominic Corrado. (Author's collection.)

Jack and Tony Tocco talk business outside the Zerilli funeral. In the years to come, Jack would be named boss and Tony consiglieri. (Author's collection.)

Family members Vito Giacalone and Tony Tocco are pictured playing golf with each other in the 1980s. (Author's collection.)

Local Mafia strong-arm Don Fragale (second from left) is pictured as the subject of an early-1980s FBI line-up. A top loan shark and debt collector for the area crime family, Fragale is the adopted stepson of notorious Detroit Mob enforcer Bernard Marchesani. The other five men in the picture were acting FBI agents, dressed in prison garb to blend in with Fragale. (Author's collection.)

Motor City Mafia soldier Leonard "Skippy" Torrice is pictured in an FBI surveillance photograph from the late 1970s. A top member of the Giacalone crew, Torrice was the crime family's lieutenant in charge of all the city's Jewish bookmakers, loan sharks, and racketeers. (Author's collection.)

This FBI mug shot is of Detroit Mob captain Vito "Billy Jack" Giacalone (left), following a late 1970s arrest. Throughout the 1970s, Giacalone drove a customized Cadillac, equipped with a secret weapon compartment (bottom) and is believed by some authorities to have been the Motor City crime family's representative at the Hoffa hit—federal agents assigned to syndicate surveillance at the time of the labor czar's disappearance claim Billy Jack was the only major area underworld figure not accounted for on the afternoon of July 30, 1975. Serving several prison sentences throughout his career on the street, Giacalone headquarters his crews operations out of the Eastern Market. (Author's collection.)

Detroit Mob loan shark and enforcer Frank Stevens is pictured in a local police mug shot from the early 1970s. A mainstay on the Motor City streets for much of the second half of the century, Stevens was one of the crime family's top non-Italian associates. (Author's collection.)

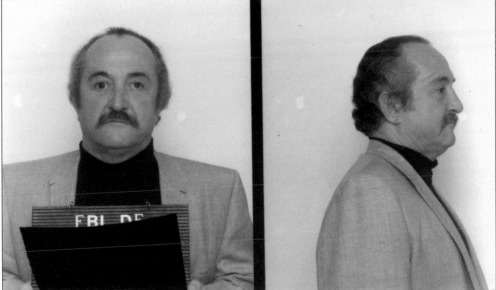

Local Mafia soldier Bernard "Bernie the Hammer" Marchesani is pictured in a FBI mug shot from the late 1970s. Marchesani, who worked directly under Detroit Mob bosses Joe Zerilli and Jack Tocco, developed a reputation as the area's most feared loan shark and gangland enforcer during his time on the Motor City streets. A fugitive from justice for over five years, Marchesani was apprehended and imprisoned, dying in jail of cancer in 1998, while still a suspect in the 1985 murder of Colleen Smith. (Author's collection.)

Notorious Detroit gangland figure and mega-bookmaker David Feldman is pictured in a DPD mug shot taken early on in the wiseguy's career. A former top associate of the Purple Gang, at the pinnacle of his underworld tenure, Feldman was considered the biggest Jewish gambling chief in the city. (Paul R. Kavieff collection.)

Motor City Mafia enforcer Danny Triglia is pictured in an FBI surveillance photograph from the mid-1970s. Brought into the local underworld at early age by his father, Joseph "Joe the Whip" Triglia, a longtime crime family lieutenant, Danny made a name for himself on the city's streets by becoming a loyal strong-arm for the Corrado brothers. (Author's collection.)

Detroit Mob enforcer Gregory "Little Pete" Katranis is pictured in an FBI surveillance photograph from the early 1970s. Katranis, whose father was long-time Mafia strong-arm Peter "Pete the Greek" Katranis, was murdered in 1972, after it was found that he had begun freelancing in the local loan sharking and extortion rackets. Mike Katranis, Little Pete's younger sibling, continued working for the syndicate following his brother's death. (Author's collection.)

Local Mafia associate Patrick "Pat the Pimp" Gatt is pictured in an FBI mug shot from the mid-1970s. Working under Detroit crime family captain Dominic "Fats" Corrado, Gatt was assigned by the Mob to head much of their interests in the area's prostitution market. (Author's collection.)

Detroit crime family soldier Joe Brooklier (left) is pictured leaving a court appearance in the 1960s. The younger brother of former Los Angles Mob boss Dominic Brooklier, Joe was a top bookie and loan shark in the area underworld. Brooklier, along with San Diego don Frank "the Bump" Bompenserio and the Licata family, represented the syndicate's close ties with the California Mafia, a relationship that has seen several soldiers switch families and many financial dividends achieved through various joint criminal ventures. (Walter Reuther Library—Wayne State University.)

Thomas "Tommy Gun" Lewis (left) and John Thomas are shown in an FBI surveillance photograph taken in the mid-1970s outside the St. Antoinette Coffee Shop, the headquarters of local Mafia captain Dominic "Fats" Corrado. Lewis worked for Corrado. (Author's collection.)

Tommy Lewis is pictured in an FBI surveillance photograph from the mid-1970s, alongside a Detroit-area call girl, while conducting business on a local street corner. Besides acting as Corrado crew muscle, Lewis was also responsible for aiding in the crime family's prostitution racket, often escorting girls to and from jobs, providing them protection, and collecting their dues. (Author's collection.)

Detroit Mob soldier Dominic Licavoli is pictured walking outside the federal courthouse in 1975 accompanied by members of law enforcement. The youngest brother of local Mafia stalwart Pete Licavoli, Dominic married the daughter of Joe Zerilli and was a mainstay on the city streets until his death in 1997. (Walter Reuther Library—Wayne State University.)

Local Mafia muscle Robert "Bobby the Tiger" La Puma (center) and August "Little Augie" Giordano (right of La Puma), leave an area diner in a mid-1970s FBI surveillance photograph. Both La Puma and Giordano, whose father was crime family soldier Sam Giordano (left) and whose cousin was St. Louis Mob boss Anthony Giordano, were considered two of the Detroit underworld's top enforcers. The Giordanos were the city's link to the Missouri crime syndicate. (Author's collection.)

Motor City Mob captains Peter Vitale and Rafaelle Quassarano are pictured in an FBI surveillance photograph from the mid-1970s, leaving an area restaurant after a meeting with underworld associates. Vitale and Quassarano, both maintained valuable ties to the East Coast Mafia and acted as the crime family's contacts with the New York underworld. (Author's collection.)

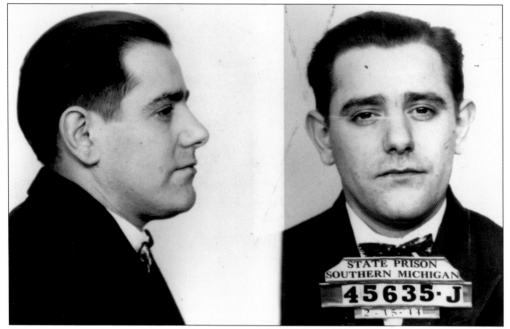

This 1940s mug shot is of James Tamer, one of the Detroit Mafia's top front-men of the 20th century. In later years, Tamer would maintain ownership of numerous gangland haunts, including the Hillcrest Country Club in Macomb County and the Aladdin Hotel and Casino in Las Vegas. Tamer was indicted in 1978 for skimming profits from the Aladdin, allegedly to funnel back to his Mob benefactors in the Motor City. (Paul R. Kavieff collection.)

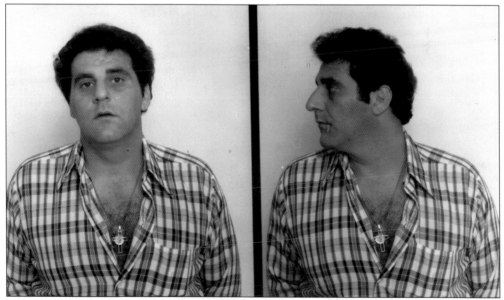

Infamous underworld horse race fixing expert and East Coast wiseguy Anthony "Tony the Fixer" Ciulla is pictured in an FBI mug shot from the mid-1970s. Ciulla, who got his start in Boston's notorious Winter Hill Gang, was sponsored by several key members of both the New York and Philadelphia Mafia crime families and came to the Motor City in 1975 to begin fixing races at the Detroit Race Course. (Author's collection.)

The Derby Bar, an area tavern located directly across the street from the Detroit Race Course, is pictured in an FBI surveillance photograph from the mid-1970s. The bar was used as Tony Ciulla and his race-fixing crew's headquarters during the years operating in the area under the protection of the Motor City Mafia crime family. (Author's collection.)

Tony Ciulla is pictured alongside associate Robert "Bobby the Teacher" Owen (left) in an FBI surveillance photograph taken outside the Derby Bar in the mid-1970s. With his highly skilled race-fixing crew in tow, Ciulla, and his gangland cronies, strong-armed jockeys, infiltrated stable maintenance, and paid off track doctors to assure the results they desired in numerous races over a two-year period. (Author's collection)

New York underworld figure and Ciulla associate Oscar "Fat Jerry" Friedman (middle) is pictured entering the Detroit Race Course and going to place a bet on a fixed race in an FBI surveillance photograph from the mid-1970s. Aligned closely with Mafia powers, Anthony "Fat Tony" Salerno, boss of New York's Genovese crime family, and Pasquale "Pat the Cat" Spirito, a soldier in the Philadelphia Mob, Friedman often delivered messages to Ciulla and various Detroit wiseguys on their behalf, as well as placed large-money wagers at the track as a front for the East Coast underworld. (Author's collection.)

Motor City Mafia soldiers Joseph Tocco (left) and his brother Nove Tocco (right) are pictured in an FBI surveillance photograph from the early 1980s, enjoying a football game with their families. Joe and Nove are the sons of local Mob lieutenant Paul Tocco, cousins to syndicate boss Jack Tocco and nephews of underboss Tony Zerilli. (Author's collection.)

Detroit Mob lawyer William Buffalino Jr., son of legendary crime family attorney William Buffalino Sr., is seen leaving a local residence in an FBI surveillance photograph taken in the late 1970s. Buffalino was married on the weekend following Jimmy Hoffa's disappearance, giving many of the nation's most prominent mafioso reason to be in the area when the decision to kill the disgruntled labor boss was made. Buffalino Jr. died in 2005 of cancer. Also pictured is area mob soldier Danny Triglia. (Author's collection.)

Frederick "Freddie the Saint" Salem (top left), Edward "Baldy" Sarkesian (top right), and Henry Allen Hilf (bottom right), the three biggest non-Italian gambling lieutenants in the Detroit underworld during the 1970s and 1980s, are pictured in an FBI surveillance photograph taken as the trio of well-connected wiseguys leave a Mob-sponsored dice game. Salem, who ran all the illegal craps games being conducted within the city limits, was often assisted by Hilf, the area's most prolific bookmaker, and Sarkesian, a local gambling expert, who served as the crime family's point man in the Las Vegas gaming industry. (Author's collection.)

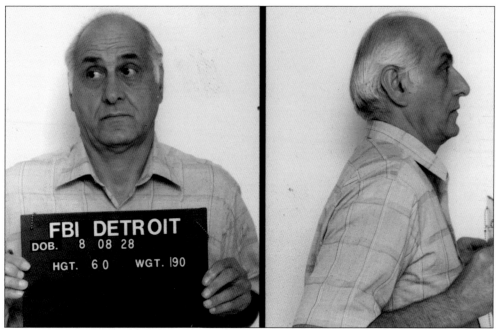

Motor City underworld leader Freddie the Saint Salem is pictured in an FBI mug shot from the 1980s. A legend in local gambling circles, Salem, who is Lebanese, was one of the biggest earners for the Detroit crime family over the past four decades, running a variety of high-stakes illegal gaming activities and a very successful sports bookmaking operation. (Author's collection.)

This FBI surveillance photograph is of Detroit Mafia street boss Tony Giacalone, entering a car driven by his son Anthony "Fat Tony" Giacalone Jr. in the early 1980s. At that time, Giacalone spent most of his days at his area headquarters, the Southfield Athletic Club, a recreational health facility owned by Giacalone crew member Leonard Shultz and his son. Giacalone, who had previously headquartered at the Home Juice Company on the east side of Detroit, was one of the most highly respected and widely revered figures in the history of the nation's underworld. (Author's collection.)

Motor City Mob lieutenant Frank Mudaro is pictured leaving a meeting with underworld associates in an FBI surveillance photograph from the 1970s. Mudaro, who was initiated into the crime family in the 1940s, was assigned to look after the syndicate's numerous investments in the local real estate market. (Author's collection.)

Local crime family associate Michael "Superfly" Kristoff is pictured in an FBI surveillance photograph taken in the late 1970s. Kristoff, whose nickname was derived from his penchant for wearing loud and flashy clothing, was an area bookmaker who often frequented Freddie Salem's headquarters at the Capitol Social Club in Oak Park. (Author's collection.)

Detroit underworld bookmaker Frank Versaci is pictured entering a local underworld gambling hot spot in an FBI surveillance photograph from the 1970s. Versaci, a close confidant of area Mob boss Jack Tocco, was one of the crime family's biggest gambling lieutenants. (Author's collection.)

Gambling chief Freddie Salem (left) is pictured delivering orders to crew members William "Buffalo Bill" Gibera (center) and Frank "New York Frankie" Inglese in an FBI surveillance photograph from the 1970s. Salem was firm yet fair and developed an impeccable reputation in the Motor City underworld, often holding after-hours casino nights at the residences of local sports celebrities Isaiah Thomas and Tommy Hearns. (Author's collection.)

This FBI aerial surveillance photograph is of Elmira Street in north Detroit where several field agents set up shop across from a residence being used as the primary location for a highly profitable dice game run by Freddie Salem and financed by the local Mafia crime family. The last house on the right side of the photograph is where the game was being held, and the last house of the center street is where the FBI watched from. (Author's collection.)

A number of FBI field agents, located directly across the street from Salem's much frequented dice game, listen in on activity transpiring at the game from audio surveillance planted in the underworld gambling domain. Acting on a court order, the residence was wired for sound by agents who infiltrated the premises and installed listening devices. (Author's collection.)

FBI field agent Robert Barenie tracks the dice game going on across the street from visual surveillance installed in the residence. Acting on a court order, the house was equipped with mini cameras placed in the ceiling, which would allow the agents keeping tabs on the gamblers to monitor their every move. (Author's collection.)

Undercover FBI agents William Randall (left) and Allen Finch are pictured right before they would precede their fellow agents into the game, parading as local gamblers, making certain the residence was primed for a successful bust. Once they were inside the house and determined the path was clear for the raid, the agents signaled their counterparts across the street to move in. (Author's collection.)

An armed squad of federal agents, with warrants in hand, raid the game, pictured here from across the street by an agent left behind to photographically document the bust. Equipped with a heavy artillery of weapons and each wearing bullet-proof vests, the agents knocked down the door of the house and entered the residence. (Author's collection.)

Here is a photograph of the bust in progress, as gun-wielding federal agents tell the members of the illegal dice game to put their hands in the air and face the wall. Notice field agent Robert Barenie (sitting with head turned), who due to a knee injury was forced to take a seat when the rest of his fellow agents frisked the suspects. (Author's collection.)

As agent Barenie (far right) continues to process the suspects, agent Dave Parker (behind Barenie) shows Freddie Salem the federal search warrant just issued and served on the premises. No stranger to the law, Salem had several gambling arrests before this and has had a few since. (Author's collection.)

This picture was taken directly after the bust of Salem's game, as agents Barenie and Parker admire the fruits of their labor with their supervisor, agent-in-charge Oscar Westerfield. The contents on the table before the agents—cash, guns, knives, gaming tools—are typical of items seized during federal raids of that form. (Author's collection.)

The head of the Detroit FBI's organized crime division from 1976 to 1985, agent Oscar Westerfield poses for a photograph in front of his desk in the late 1970s. Finishing his career in the Tampa FBI office, Westerfield is currently semi-retired and works in the private security field. (Author's collection.)

Detroit underworld figure Joe Mirabile is pictured entering a local gambling den in an FBI surveillance photograph from the 1970s. Mirabile, who was the son of former Mob bigwig Anthony "Papa Tony" Mirabile, the crime family's inaugural representative on the West Coast, was believed by authorities to have been an associate of Joe Matrenga, his father's replacement as the syndicate's captain in charge of California. (Author's collection.)

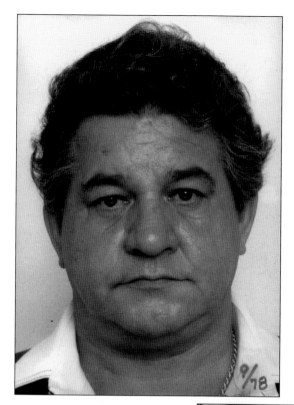

Local Mob associate Al Hady is pictured in an FBI mug shot from 1978. A loyal and trusted member of Vito "Billy Jake" Giacalone's crew, Hady acted as Billy Jack's top emissary on the area's streets, dispensing orders and making collections on his behalf. (Author's collection.)

Motor City crime family chief Vincent Meli is pictured in an FBI surveillance photograph from the 1970s. Married to the daughter of former Detroit Mafia captain Santo "Cockeyed Sam" Perrone, Meli owned a local record company and maintained key ties in the area's steel hauling and labor communities. In the 1990s, Meli was promoted to acting underboss when a majority of the syndicate was jailed on racketeering charges. (Author's collection.)

Seven

THE NEW GENERATION

With the 1970s coming to a close and the high-profile antics of the Hoffa situation in the crime family's rear-view mirror, freshly minted Detroit Mob don Jack Tocco made a visibly conscious effort to peal back the local Mafia's presence on the city's streets, taking his administration underground, trying to limit the syndicate's exposure to federal prosecution as much as possible. Tocco's edict paid quick dividends, the family removed itself from the area's lucrative but high-risk drug industry and was quickly replaced by a series of prolific and violent black drug cartels that for a period of close to 10 years littered the Motor City with cheap narcotics and heavy bloodshed. By the end of the decade, these new-breed gangsters, led by the likes of drug lords Milton "Butch" Jones, Richard "Maseratti Rick" Carter, and Richard "White Boy Rick" Wershe, had effectively removed the Detroit Mafia from the media spotlight, eliminating each other in a barrage of death, gunfire, and large-scale legal battles that in the end paved the way for the Italian Mob's return to the streets in the 1990s.

No longer plying their trade in the city's high-risk narcotic racket, Tocco refocused the crime family's energy into building up their gambling, loan sharking, and extortion operations into well-oiled money machines, exceeding syndicate profit margins from previous decades and successfully remaining off the government's radar. At the start of the 1990s, although the local Mafia was smaller in size, its power and prestige remained unmatched in gangland circles across the country until a wide-spanning indictment in 1996, charging the entire Motor City Mob hierarchy in an extensive RICO case (spawning from an investigation federal authorities named Operation Game Tax), ravished the city's underworld. Jack Tocco and his second-in-command, Anthony Zerilli, were both eventually brought down by the federal government, convicted, and jailed on the charges.

Several area Mafia luminaries enjoy a day on the links, playing golf at the Hillcrest Country Club in the early 1980s while being photographed by an FBI surveillance team. Pictured about to tee off on the first hole are (left to right) crime family captain Anthony Corrado; boss Jack Tocco, who owned part of the golf course itself; soon-to-be consiglieri Anthony Tocco; Vito's son Jack (back turned to the camera); then consiglieri Michael Polizzi; and top Mob lieutenant Vito Giacalone. In the years since, Polizzi was demoted for the actions of his son, and replaced as syndicate consiglieri by Anthony Tocco. (Author's collection.)

This photograph is of FBI agent Mike Carone (facing camera) talking to Detroit Mob gambling chief Henry Allen Hilf (backed turned) in the 1990s, shortly after Carone and several other agents busted into his suburban condominium to serve him with a search warrant. Since the raid took place in the morning, Hilf, known on the streets as "the General," is in a bathrobe, having not even risen from bed when the agents came knocking. (Author's collection.)

Local underworld associate Eugene Baratta is pictured getting into his automobile in an FBI surveillance photograph from the 1980s. A son-in-law to area Mafia boss Jack Tocco, Baratta is alleged by authorities to have often delivered messages to family members and various Mob soldiers on behalf of the godfather. (Author's collection.)

Detroit Mob soldier and turncoat Nove Tocco is pictured in an FBI mug shot taken after his March 1996 arrest as part of Operation Game Tax. Following being taken into custody, Tocco, whose uncle is underboss Anthony Zerilli and whose cousin is local Mafia godfather Jack Tocco, became the first member of the city's crime family to defect to the government and testify against the syndicate in court. (Author's collection.)

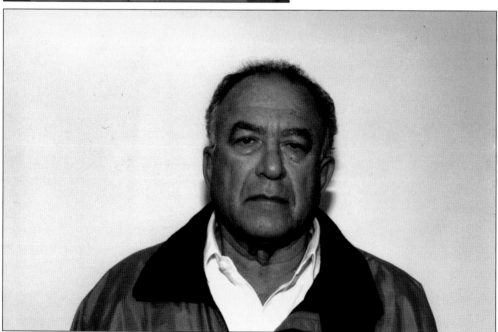

Motor City Mafia don Jack Tocco is seen in an FBI mug shot taken following his arrest in March 1996 on federal racketeering charges, in which the government alleged that Tocco was boss of the Detroit Mob. Convicted and jailed, Tocco served a remarkably light two-year prison sentence and then resumed his post as overlord of the city's streets. (Author's collection.)

Local Mob underboss Anthony Zerilli is pictured in an FBI mug shot taken after his arrest on federal racketeering charges in March 1996. Caught on tape commanding underlings to use violence against uncooperative street merchants, Zerilli was convicted and imprisoned when the government successfully proved to a jury that Zerilli was the second-highest ranking Mafia figure in the city of Detroit. (Author's collection.)

Detroit crime family consiglieri Anthony Tocco is pictured in an FBI mug shot following his March 1996 arrest on federal racketeering charges. The only member of the local Mafia leadership hierarchy not convicted in the case, Tony, known to friends as "Tawn," assumed the role of acting boss and took control of the syndicate's day-to-day affairs while his brother was in prison. (Author's collection.)

Former area Mafia captain Anthony Corrado is seen in an FBI mug shot taken after his March 1996 arrest on federal racketeering charges stemming from the government's Operation Game Tax. Convicted and jailed in the case, Tony the Bull died in prison in 2002 of heart failure. (Author's collection.)

Motor City underworld legend Anthony Giacalone is seen in an FBI mug shot taken after his arrest in March 1996 on federal racketeering charges. Alleged to be in charge of all of the Detroit crime family's activity on the local streets, Tony Jack was spared trial due to his failing health. (Author's collection.)

Detroit Mafia captain Vito Giacalone (left) is pictured in the early 1990s as the best man at crew member Frank Bommarito's (second from right) wedding. Indicted alongside the rest of the local Mob power structure in the 1996 Operation Game Tax bust, Giacalone plead guilty to lesser charges in 1998 and astonishingly, as a part of his plea agreement, admitted in open court to the existence of the Mafia and his membership within. (Author's collection.)

The two Giacalone brothers, Anthony (center) and Vito (right of Anthony), and all their respective sons are seen in a professional photograph taken at a lavish party celebrating Tony Jack's wedding anniversary, which took place in the early 1990s at the Ritz-Carlton Hotel in Dearborn. (Author's collection.)

Detroit Piston point guard Isaiah Thomas is pictured in the summer of 1981 at the press conference welcoming the NBA first-round pick to town after the franchise selected him third overall in that year's draft. In 1990, news reports broke of Thomas's alleged ties to the local crime syndicate, his involvement in high-stakes illegal dice games that took place at the Hall of Fame player's mansion in the suburbs (pictured below) and suspicious check-cashing activity exhibited by the Motor City icon in months previous. Subpoenaed to appear before a federal grand jury investigating a nationwide sports gambling ring being run out of Detroit by the Tocco crime family, Thomas was asked questions regarding the over $40,000 in checks he had cashed through a neighborhood grocery, the late-night gambling affairs that took place in his home, and his personal betting habits, before being dismissed from his testimony and not charged in the subsequent indictment. (Above, Wayne State University; below, author's collection.)

Local underworld figure Emmett Denha is pictured in an FBI mug shot from the 1980s. Denha, who was charged in the wide-scale investigation involving Thomas, was Thomas's best friend and owner of the grocery store where Thomas had cashed the subpoenaed checks; Thomas cashed hundreds of thousands of dollars of checks at the store, some $40,000 of which were examined by the grand jury. In the spring of 1990, Mark Auguire, Thomas's boyhood pal and Piston teammate, became so worried about his friend's gambling habits and Mob connections that he met with an FBI agent to voice his concerns. (Author's collection.)

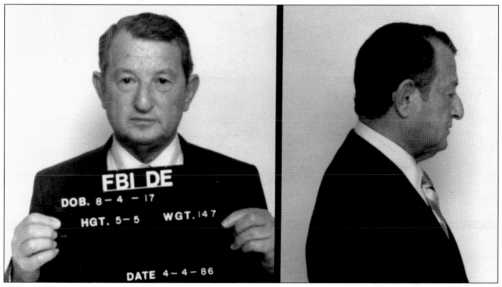

Detroit Mob lieutenant Leonard Schultz is pictured in a 1980s FBI mug shot. A member of Anthony Giacalone's crew, Schultz was Tony Jack's top emissary to the local labor unions and owner and operator of his headquarters, the Southfield Athletic Club. (Author's collection.)

Former boxing world champion Thomas "Tommy the Hitman" Hearns is pictured at a press conference in the early 1980s. Hearns rose to prominence and captured the city's heart in his run to championship glory in the late 1970s and 1980s. A legend in the pantheon of Detroit sports greats, Hearns was subpoenaed to testify at a deposition in 1991, investigating a shooting death that took place at his suburban estate that involved his brother. The heavily lauded Motor City pugilist admitted to holding and participating in underworld-backed dice games at his palatial estate in Southfield that were run and financed by the local Mob syndicate. (Walter Reuther Library—Wayne State University.)

Eight

TODAY, THE FUTURE, AND BEYOND

Living beneath the surface of the city streets, less acknowledged than ever before in their history, the Detroit Mafia still exists, dominating and profiting from the area's numerous vice rackets just like they have in the past. Serving two years in prison for his late-1990s racketeering conviction, local crime family boss Jack Tocco emerged from jail in 2002 and reassumed his position atop the city's Mob hierarchy, determined to live out his remaining years a free man, but not yet ready to relinquish control of his vast criminal empire. While underboss Anthony Zerilli remains incarcerated until 2008, Tocco delegates responsibilities and orders through his brother and syndicate consiglieri Anthony "Tony T" Tocco, as well as street boss Vito "Billy Jack" Giacalone, and top captains Jack "Jackie the Kid" Giacalone, Frank "Frankie the Bomb" Bommarito, and Anthony "Chicago Tony" La Piana, keeping a close eye on his family's affairs from his mansion in the suburbs.

Significantly reduced in numbers—recent FBI accounts place Motor City Mafia membership at roughly 25 made members with about 75–100 associates, compared to nearly triple that in the 1970s—as well as headline grabbing exploits, there have only been five Mob-related homicides in the last two decades, the Detroit crime family is the most functional, healthy, and financially profitable Mafia syndicate in the entire country. While other regional Mob families have been destroyed from within by internal squabbling and government defection, the Motor City Mafia has only had one made member ever turn federal witness, an astronomical feat considering the current underworld landscape. The Detroit faction of La Cosa Nostra remains a silent but ultimately very real and deadly presence in American gangland culture while exhibiting no signs of slowing down. And, although membership is aging, a new generation will eventually ascend to take the reins of the local Mafia and lead the storied crime family into the future and, most likely, beyond.

Detroit Mafia captain Jack "Jackie the Kid" Giacalone is seen in an FBI photograph taken of him in the late 1980s. The son of Vito Giacalone, Jackie the Kid is currently the syndicate's lieutenant in charge of all gambling activity taking place within the city. Former owner of Farm Fresh Produce, at one time eastern market's largest wholesale produce company, the younger Giacalone was made in 1985 and upped to captain status in the 1990s. Authorities speculate he will most likely become the next boss of the Motor City crime family. (Author's collection.)

Motor City Mob lieutenant Anthony "Fat Tony" Giacalone Jr. is seen in an FBI photograph taken of him in the late 1990s. Oldest son of former Mafia street boss Anthony Giacalone Sr., Fat Tony was named captain of his father's crew, following his death in 2001. (Author's collection.)

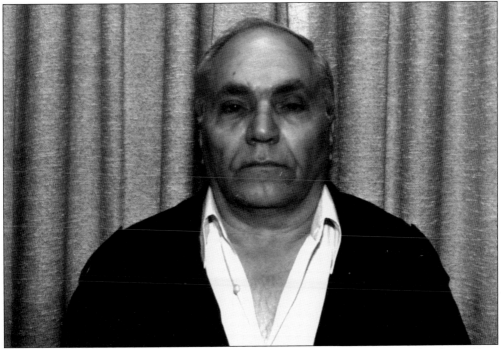

Longtime area gangland figure Frank Bommarito is seen in an FBI photograph taken of him in the late 1990s. A loyal soldier in the Detroit Mafia since the 1970s, Bommarito was recently made a captain after Vito Giacalone was promoted to street boss. (Author's collection.)

Local Mafia soldier Carlo Bommarito is shown in an FBI mug shot taken in the late 1990s. Initiated into the crime family in 1995 by Detroit don Jack Tocco at the city's last known making ceremony, Bommarito, whose father is Motor City wiseguy Frank Bommarito, is one of the youngest members of the area Mob syndicate. (Author's collection.)

Current Motor City Mafia captain Anthony "Chicago Tony" La Piana is pictured in an FBI surveillance photograph from the mid-1980s. A transplant from the Windy City, La Piana is the son-in-law of local Mob heavy Vincent Meli, as well as a suspect in the 1984 death of union power Ralph Proctor. Acting as the Detroit underworld's liaison to the Chicago crime syndicate, La Piana is viewed by authorities as one of the possible successors to Jack Tocco and the crime family throne. (Author's collection.)

Detroit crime family soldier Paul "Big Paulie" Corrado, son of Fats Corrado, is shown in an FBI mug shot taken of him in the late 1990s. Often confused with his first cousin Paul "Cousin Paulie" Corrado, another member of the local Mafia syndicate, Big Paulie was convicted in 1998 in the Operation Game Tax case, on the testimony of his gangland business partner, Nove Tocco. (Author's collection.)

Vito Giacalone is pictured alongside his older brother Tony in a family photograph from the early 1990s. After Tony died in 2001, Vito was named to succeed him as the crime family's street boss, a position he holds to this day. (Author's collection.)

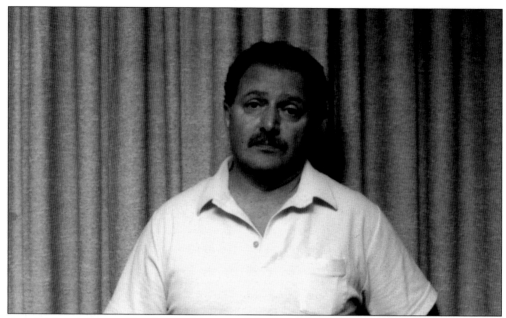

Area Mob associate and local strip club owner John Jarjosa is shown in an FBI mug shot taken in the mid-1990s, following his arrest for his involvement in the Operation Game Tax investigation. Jailed on the charges, along with a number of other top members of the Detroit underworld, Jarjosa's son John Jarjosa Jr. was murdered in 2001. (Author's collection.)

Motor City underworld mainstay Henry A. Hilf (left) is shown in an FBI surveillance photograph taken of him sitting courtside at a Detroit Pistons home game with an associate. Serving jail time for an early 1990s gambling bust and a late 1990s parole violation, Hilf is still considered the area's top bookmaker. (Author's collection.)

Detroit Mafia lieutenant Peter Tocco is pictured in an FBI surveillance photograph from the early 1980s. A nephew of local Mob boss Jack Tocco, Peter was indicted, along with Jack Giacalone, in March 2006 on federal gambling charges. (Author's collection.)

Jack Giacalone is pictured alongside his father's former right-hand man, Al Hady, in an FBI surveillance photograph taken of them playing a round of golf in the 1980s. Along with fellow syndicate captains Anthony La Piana and Anthony Giacalone Jr., Jackie the Kid will be looked upon to lead the crime family into the next generation. (Author's collection.)

A rare photograph taken at a local underworld social event in the late 1990s shows the entire modern-day Detroit Mafia hierarchy with their wives enjoying a night on the town. Area godfather Jack Tocco (standing) is joined by acting underboss Vincent Meli (right of Tocco) and consiglieri Tony Tocco (next to Meli), as well as former captain Anthony Corrado (left of Tocco) and the syndicate's most-tenured member, Rafaelle Quassarano. Tocco, who along with his entire inner-circle, received a college business degree and is currently the nation's longest reigning Mob boss, serving nearly 30 years at the helm of the area's crime family. (Author's collection.)

BIBLIOGRAPHY

Abadinsky, Howard. *Organized Crime*. Chicago: Nelson-Hill Publishers, 1997.

Brandt, Charles. *"I Heard You Paint Houses": Frank "the Irishman" Sheeran and the Inside Story of the Mafia, the Teamsters, and the Last Ride of Jimmy Hoffa*. Hanover, NH: The Steerforth Press, 2004.

Kavieff, Paul R. *The Purple Gang: Organized In Detroit 1910–1040*. Fort Lee, NJ: Barricade Books, 2000.

———. *The Violent Years: Prohibition and the Detroit Mobs*. Fort Lee, NJ: Barricade Books, 2001.

Keteyian, Armen, Harvey Araton, and Martin F. Dardis. *Money Players: Days and Nights Inside the New NBA*. New York: Pocket Books, 1997.

Maas, Peter. *The Valachi Papers*. New York: Perennial Press, 1968.

Moldea, Dan B. The *Hoffa Wars: The Rise and Fall of Jimmy Hoffa*. New York: Schlopsky Press, 1993.

Porrello, Rick. *To Kill the Irishman: The War That Crippled the Mafia*. Cleveland, OH: Next Hat Press, 1998.

Reid, Ed. *The Anatomy of Organized Crime In America: The Grim Reapers*. Chicago: Henry-Regnery, 1968.

Discover Thousands of Local History Books
Featuring Millions of Vintage Images

Arcadia Publishing, the leading local history publisher in the United States, is committed to making history accessible and meaningful through publishing books that celebrate and preserve the heritage of America's people and places.

Find more books like this at
www.arcadiapublishing.com

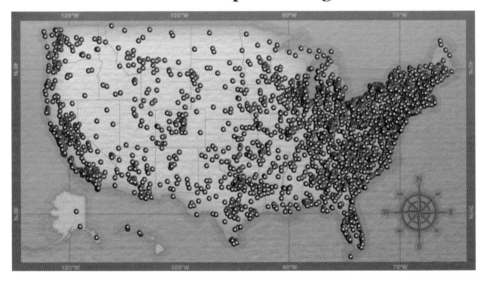

Search for your hometown history, your old stomping grounds, and even your favorite sports team.

Consistent with our mission to preserve history on a local level, this book was printed in South Carolina on American-made paper and manufactured entirely in the United States. Products carrying the accredited Forest Stewardship Council (FSC) label are printed on 100 percent FSC-certified paper.

MADE IN THE USA